Pray the Answer
Not the Problem

CAROL GRAHAM

For more information about this title or to order other books
and/or electronic media, contact the publisher:
carolg4589@gmail.com

Printed in the USA

979-8-9887848-0-7 (paperback)
979-8-9887848-1-4 (ebook)

Interior & Cover design by
Dan & Darlene Swanson
www.van-garde.com

Contents

Introduction

PRAY THE ANSWER. Just that simple.

Have you ever shaken your fist at God, or had tears wet your pillow night after night? But still no answer to your prayers.

Many engage in an exhausting effort wondering if God will ever answer and whether or not He is listening or even cares.

Is there a secret to the effective way to pray? No secret, but rather, a sure path to present petitions, to declare what is true, and to proclaim God's Word that already states the outcome. Many engage in an exhausting effort, wondering if God will ever answer, whether He is listening or even cares.

Through this book, I present real-life stories to illustrate the powerful way in which God showcases His miracles. These stories are stand-alone miracles you will want to share with others who need answers to their situation.

My dream to someday be a mommy began as a little girl. In my twenties, the ovarian cancer diagnosis shattered that dream and threatened my life as well. I needed God's healing — for me and my husband. And yes, I desperately wanted a child.

As I laid on the sofa in intense pain, God revealed to me that my healing was already promised. My job was to believe it. To thank Him for it. To stand strong in my belief and to ward off doubt and fear by quoting His promise. The more I quoted the promise in Luke 1:45 "Blessed is she who believed, for there will be a fulfillment of those things which were told her from the Lord" the more I believed it and the more excited I became.

I waited 14 years to become pregnant and could have stopped believing the promise at any time. I could have stopped at 13 years or one year. Would that have made a difference? Most definitely. Was I willing to take that chance? Never. Did I ask God why it was taking so long? No. I did not. I chose to believe God's Word. That was my commission.

My contract with God was a signed one. He promised. I believed. He signed it with the blood of His Son, Jesus. There was no room for doubt. God's timing is perfect. Every. Time.

God made the promise, and He is a God of His Word. I hung on. The more I proclaimed and thanked God for my healing, the more excited I became. I did not doubt it.

Realize deeply, God never has a different plan or opinion. What He has promised in His Word, you can bank on. His will is His Word. Period.

Sadly, sometimes it is easier to believe the lies that scream at us than to believe the truth God gives us. Then we conjure up reasons why our prayers may not be answered.

Have you ever asked yourself any of these questions: "How do I know it is God's will to heal me? What if He has other plans?"

Our prayers need to be a statement of faith instead of unbelief, which is simply praying the answer instead of the problem. They need to fall into line with that truth, not with the circumstances around us or the lies we could so easily believe.

Pray the Answer.....Instead of the Problem explains various types of prayer including:

- How to pray when you need a miracle
- How to understand God's will
- What if God says "No"
- The prayer of agreement
- What to do when your answer is taking too long
- Stepping out of your comfort zone
- The prayer that unlocks heaven
- Understanding your authority

Each chapter is explained by illustrating a miracle story that can be used as stand-alone stories to share.

To get the greatest benefit from this book of miracles answer the questions after each chapter. This will both motivate and inspire you to make some important changes in your prayer life and begin to see the manifestation of the miracles for which you had hoped.

When we change our thinking from doubt, worry, and confusion to the assured belief of God's goodness in our lives, everything changes — our health, our finances, our Christian walk.

This is not wishful thinking but the confident expectation of God's goodness!

Chapter 1
When You Need a Miracle

THE SPECIALIST SEATED across from me raised his eyebrows, "Ovarian cancer is serious," he said with no emotion, "you have two choices, hysterectomy or death."

That's it? Those two horrible choices? Years of pain and a desperate search for the best doctor had brought me to this renowned specialist. And this was his solution?

How could he be so insensitive? Anger started to build in me. But his words did not intimidate me.

Swallowing hard, I said, "I do not accept those choices."

His frown framed the fire in his eyes. Had I challenged him? Rising from his chair, he leaned over his desk. He pointed his finger inches from my face.

"Then, lady, go home. Suffer. And die." His spit splattered my cheek when he spoke.

I clutched the armrests of the wooden chair, my heart beat fast and my face grew hot as I stood up and leaned toward him. In a loud voice, enunciating each syllable clearly, I said through gritted teeth, "I will walk in here pregnant one day." I spun around and marched out the door.

Once out of his office, I took a deep breath. What did I just do? My hands shook, tears welled up and remorse attacked me. Why did I say that?

That specialist was my last hope. Or was he?

My anger in the doctor's office brought on worry and anxious thoughts.

Will this disease kill me? How can I face another diagnosis of this magnitude?

Years earlier another specialist said, "There is one chance in a million of getting pregnant because of damage due to your previous illnesses." It seemed hopeless.

I had a sister who died at the age of twelve from rheumatic fever four years before I was born. My parents prayed for another child and God granted their request — me.

However, I was a sickly child and when I was only nine months old, I stopped breathing for twenty minutes and lay lifeless in my crib. My parents knew God had gifted me to them and their faith was not going to allow another child to be taken. They chose to believe in God for a miracle and not allow this to overtake them.

The same faith my parents had for my healing as a baby began to build up inside me and confirmed I would be victorious in this conflict. God had to have an answer for me; I was determined to find it.

But was my sheer determination enough? At times belief seemed to fade. What did not fade was the weight of the cancer diagnosis which hung over me.

In those anxious moments of fear, I was sure my only hope for survival was the One I knew well. My Healer. My Source of confidence. Doctors had no answers. But God did.

Knowing that God had the answers helped strengthen me on the days when believing was difficult. But I needed to maintain my faith and trust God was true to His Word. Standing on that truth, I repeated to God over and over again, "I know You'll never fail me. I know your promises are true." His answer would come. And I vowed to find it no matter what.

Embracing the truth my father instilled in me, I knew I would triumph: Whatever I would feed would grow and whatever I would starve eventually would fade and die. I could feed my fears or feed my faith. The choice was mine. I kept that truth in front of me, remembering in the dark what I had learned in the light.

My faith was unwavering. I leaned on God's wisdom to guide me while I waited for the manifestation of my healing. After the visit to the doctor and contrary to my friends' warnings, I weaned myself from all medications. Though a risky step to take, I took it because the medications made me feel worse and did not appear to be working. The medical profession did not have answers and gave me no hope. Hysterectomy, out of the question. Death — it was not yet my time.

God's timing was perfect and while I waited, I prayed. I searched the Bible. I looked for answers. One thread that would be mine and mine alone. A light I could cling to in the dark days.

After days of lying on the sofa in extreme pain begging God for an answer, that light came on. God spoke to my heart. His voice was so loud it seemed audible. He gave me a simple, yet profound, promise. I chose to believe it. This specific, unique verse changed the direction of my life: "Blessed is she who believed: for there will be a fulfillment of those things which were told her from the Lord." Luke 1:45

My heart skipped a beat. Joy welled up inside of me. A new expectation was born. My campaign began with this truth to receive the fulfillment of that promise of healing and a baby. No matter how severe the pain got, I would praise God for that scripture verse. I put it on post-it notes throughout the house. Every time I saw it, I read it out loud because God's Word claims, "Faith comes by hearing and hearing by the Word of God" Romans 10:17. The more I repeated it, the stronger my faith became.

I knew this was God's promise. My focus had to remain on two things: healing and His promise.

Years earlier, the doctors told my husband: "Clayton, you have had two surgeries, and we have tried every medication available to help you produce mature sperm. I'm sorry but it is a hopeless situation. You will never father a child."

Never? God cannot lie. He is incapable of it. God knew the end of my story. All I had to do was to trust Him at His Word and He would bring it to pass. He gave me a promise. His Word is true. My job was to believe Him.

Three weeks after my doctor's visit, a neighbor called. She knew I had been extremely ill and wondered if I would be interested in attending a food supplement demonstration in her home. It did not interest me in the least, but, as a good neighbor, I agreed to attend.

That evening became the turning point. It changed the way I thought about food and convinced me I needed to supplement my diet to improve my health. It was part of the answer I had been searching for. God had orchestrated this event.

I had always assumed we received all the nutrition we needed from our food. At the meeting I learned how our food is processed and how our soil is depleted of nutrients. I began taking courses on nutrition and learned the importance of destroying the toxins in my home, especially from household cleaners.

Although that meeting changed my lifestyle I wondered if it would be enough to destroy cancer. However, my health started to improve dramatically after starting food supplements. My energy level was rising. My skin cleared and my attitude grew cheerful. Before the cancer diagnosis, it was confirmed that I had rheumatoid arthritis throughout my body. A few months after I changed my diet, the arthritic pain and inflammation decreased. I had better mobility, which was an outward sign of how my body was changing on the inside. Taking various pain medications for years, I had developed ulcers. But now I could eat anything I desired without a painful reaction. Something major was happening. I was no longer suffering from medication side effects including dizziness, depression, and headaches.

I understood nutrition would fight the monster in my body, but I needed a miracle to get pregnant. Not just a miracle in my own body but my husband's as well. I knew only God could create life.

My husband walked with me through each step. Our faith replaced all traces of bleakness. That was how our story began. We refused to stop believing and we supported each other. The path was long and learning-rich.

On the days I leaned toward questioning if we would ever be parents, my life partner would not accept any negative talk. He quoted the scripture God had given me and believed with me for our mutual healing. The diagnosis of his sterility did not affect him. He stood strong in the face of what would seem a hopeless situation.

Fourteen years of perseverance dragged on, but I knew that one day there would be a fulfillment of that scripture the Lord promised in His Word, years earlier. "Blessed is she who believed: for there will be a fulfillment of those things which were told her from the Lord" Luke 1:45.

I realized that recent positive changes in my body were undeniable and I assumed I was pregnant. I waited two months before seeing my current physician to confirm it.

"Carol, you are going to have a baby." My doctor glowed as she told me.

Tears were instant as I jumped up to hug my doctor. I had waited for more than fourteen years to hear those words. My husband was in the waiting room, but I didn't have to utter one word when I approached him. We hugged. We cried.

"You realize you need to see the specialist who told you it would never happen," Clayton stated cautiously.

"Realize? I can't wait. He needs to hear about this miracle. I promised him I would return to his office pregnant."

I nervously dialed the specialist's office. The receptionist questioned me, so I had to think quickly.

"It's been years since you have seen this doctor. Why are you making an appointment now?"

"I need to schedule a complete physical. The doctor told me to see him if my condition changed." I was stretching the truth a bit.

A week later I waited in that doctor's office for the blood and urine test results.

"I'll be back in a moment," the nurse said.

She had no idea about the impact her words had on me. I had waited over a decade; I could wait a few more minutes.

Those few minutes felt like time stood still. I watched the clock. Each minute seemed like an eternity. My muscles tightened and my stomach churned. I could barely contain the anticipation. After 27 endless minutes, the door opened.

Instead of the nurse, the doctor walked in, his face cold as his words stumbled out. He did not make eye contact.

"Carol, I am sorry to inform you, but you are very pregnant."

"Yes doctor," my words came out quickly, "I am fully aware that you are sorry to inform me."

Deep inside I assumed he would be happy for me as I wanted to share my miracle with him. But I assume he remembered the words he shouted over a decade ago which made this encounter uncomfortable for him.

There was nothing more to say. I smiled as I prepared to leave his office, but his question startled me. "Who's the father?"

Of course, he could ask that question. My husband who was diagnosed as sterile fathered our child. I chose not to answer. The negativity in the room did not allow me to share my belief in miracles. I walked out, my head held high, thanking God for answered prayer.

For this doctor and most, miracles, healing, and restoration are common impossibilities. This mindset becomes the barrier to believing prayer is effective.

In this book, I will show you how to remove those barriers. You will learn the vital difference between praying and believing.

You might have experienced discouragement when your prayers were not answered. Like many, you wonder if prayer even works.

For that reason, it is important to know that there are keys to receiving answers when we pray. We will go through the steps together and learn those prayer secrets.

1. **What does it mean to stand on the Word?**
Standing on the Word of God means that you understand God's Word is the final authority. Circumstances that bring doubt have no place here. It means to refuse to doubt or to believe what you see but to meditate on what Scripture God has promised you.

2. **Where does faith come from? Can you pray for more faith?**
    A. Faith comes by hearing and hearing by the Word of God. Our faith builds as we 'say' the scripture — hear it, repeat it until it is deep in our hearts (our spirit). Romans 10:17

    B. God gives each of us a measure of faith. It is given to us. We do not need to pray for more.

3. Do you struggle with doubt or find a solution from the Bible when faced with a crisis?

Start a journal of your prayer requests, what scriptures you applied each time, and how God answered your prayers.

Chapter 2
What is Prayer?

UNDERSTANDING DIFFERENT TYPES of prayer and how to pray in any situation is illustrated in this story.

One Sunday morning when my children were young, I had an intense sense we were to attend a different church that day. I recognized the prompting from the Holy Spirit and was eager to find out what God had planned.

"Mom why aren't we going to my Sunday school today?" my eight-year-old asked from the back seat.

How do I explain a prompting from the Holy Spirit to a child? I decided to wait before answering him. I had learned to obey my inner voice, trusting that in time, God would reveal the reason. It would be a great lesson to teach my children.

That morning, the pastor announced their youth leader, Peter, had suffered an unbearable stomach ache a few weeks earlier. It was determined he had a plugged bile duct and emergency surgery had been performed. But it was too late. Peter was full of cancer and beyond any medical help or the possibility of recovery. The prognosis was he would survive only a few days. Peter was 32 years old with a small child and another baby on the way.

The pastor prayed for God's will to be performed in this situation. Immediately, I knew why God sent me to this church. He wanted me to minister to Peter and his family.

"Why would you ask me to go to the hospital to pray for this man, Lord? I don't know anyone in this congregation."

Silence.

I asked again, "How do you expect me to get access to the ICU?"

Silence.

"There are capable people in this congregation. What if they laugh at me when I get to the hospital? What if they won't let me see him?"

My thoughts were interrupted when my young son leaned over and said, "You gonna go pray for him, Mommy?"

At ten years old when I was praying at the altar in my father's church, I promised God I would always do what He asked me to do — no matter what. Never forgetting the impact that vow made on me, I taught my children to be available and obedient when God speaks to their hearts.

Was it ever easy? Obedience has a price attached to it. It requires courage, humility, and trust. But the results offset any issues that evolved from stepping out of your comfort zone.

I nodded and smiled when my son asked that question. "Yes, honey, I will go to the hospital to pray for him."

After the congregation prayed, the pastor said Peter's entire family was visiting from out of town in preparation for his funeral. If anyone wanted to pay their respects to the family, they needed to do it promptly. Immediately, a fervor burned within, and hesitation lifted — a combination of excitement and fear.

As I approached the hospital I wondered if I would be allowed access to the ICU, especially with Peter's family present. I imagined only pastors and family would be permitted to visit Peter's room. God had to make the way.

Thoughts raced in my head, repeating why I should turn around and go home. But I fought them by focusing on the reason God sent me there. A miracle would unfold.

As the elevator door opened, I could easily see the lounge area where twenty-five people spoke in soft tones and one of them was a pregnant young woman.

"Hi, are you Peter's wife?" I asked her.

Her eyebrows lifted and her bloodshot eyes stared at me, "Yes, I am. Do I know you?"

I smiled at her and asked, "Could I speak with you in private in the hallway?"

She glanced at her family, and they looked perplexed, but she followed me into the hallway.

I took both of her hands in mine. Looking deeply into her eyes I said, "I believe in miracles and have seen many of them in my life. As a baby, I died, but my father's prayers raised me from that deathbed. God also healed me of cancer as a young woman. I am confident God wants to heal your husband. He cares about you, and He sent me here to pray for Peter. Would you be willing to give me the opportunity?"

In a loud whisper, she said "Yes!"

This surprised me as I assumed the hurdles her family might put up would stop her from agreeing to prayer. I wanted her to be certain, so I suggested she speak with them first.

My thoughts continued, "It is not too late to turn around. They don't know your name. Just leave."

Underscoring those thoughts were the quiet comments I heard from the family a few feet away. "You don't know her. She could be some kind of kook! Who is she? Why is she here? Why would we want to give Peter or you any false hope?"

After a couple of minutes, twelve people approached me to say I could pray for Peter. "But we are going to be there 'just in case'."

I was not sure what they meant but it felt like they were putting pressure on me to accomplish something. What they did not realize was they were about to witness a miracle.

Walking into Peter's room there was an overwhelming stench of death. As I looked at the shell of a man lying on that bed, compassion filled my heart. Peter's mother was sitting next to his bed, and she glared at me. I imagined she wondered what a stranger was doing in this private family setting. The room felt cold, and I sensed the unbelief as they prepared for Peter's funeral. I interrupted those plans.

I approached Peter's bed. He seemed weak and unresponsive. I took his hand in mine.

"Peter, God sent me here to pray for you today," I said calmly. "I firmly believe He wants you whole and healed."

The tension in the room thickened. At this point, I thought someone might ask me to leave. But everyone was silent.

I continued, "Peter when Jesus died on the cross not only did He die for our salvation and eternal life, but He also took the brutal stripes on his body for our healing."

Peter's hand was still limp in my grip. "Peter, it is God's desire you live a full life and help your wife raise your children. He wants to set you free from cancer raging inside of you."

The tension in the room continued and there was no indication from Peter that he knew I was there.

"Peter, if you would like me to pray for you and receive healing today, please open your eyes."

There was a dead hush in the room except for a slight gasp from someone behind me. I imagined they were concerned about giving Peter or his wife false hope.

I waited many seconds and Peter's eyes quivered, opening slightly and quickly closing again.

Whenever God has asked me to pray for someone, I rarely have any idea what I will say until I open my mouth to speak. This is part of understanding what prayer is and how to pray in any given situation. It is learning how to listen to your spirit where we hear God's voice, instead of devising a plan in your mind. We will discuss this throughout this book.

God must honor His Word. He cannot lie. It was my responsibility to pray the answer found in the Bible, and not pray the problem. It is that simple. All the answers we need for any given situation are in the Word of God. When we find the answer to our problem, we pray it by voicing it. Basic, simple truth.

As I closed my eyes to pray, Romans 8:11 came to me and I recited it out loud. *"But if the Spirit of Him who raised Jesus from the dead dwells in you, He who raised Christ Jesus from the dead will also give you life to your mortal bodies through His Spirit who dwells in you."*

That is all I said. I paused. Then I repeated it the second time, a bit louder.

There was a flutter in Peter's closed eyes. I knew he was trying to respond.

I repeated it the third time. I prayed nothing else. I did not ask for Peter's healing. I only spoke the truth from God's promises. Peter opened his eyes. By the sixth time, he squeezed my hand as he looked directly into my eyes.

A few more times and he was smiling at me. Someone in the room started clapping their hands. I could hear sobs behind me.

I raised my eyes toward heaven and prayed, "Thank you, Heavenly Father, for the miracle we just witnessed. We praise You for healing Peter and for honoring Your Word. We choose to believe the promise in the Bible that healing is ours."

I smiled. The family needed their privacy.

"See you in church Sunday," I said as I left the room quickly.

Two men came running down the hall after me and asked my name, what church I attended, and why I came there today.

I told them the only thing that mattered was God asked me to be there and I was obedient. He did the rest.

Peter's story does not end here. We will explore it further in chapter three as well as another miracle God performed because of my obedience. I did not ask for nor expect to be rewarded but God confirmed He was pleased.

But first, let us look at what prayer is, and the authority God has given to each of us.

1. How can we be sure God hears our prayers?

When we pray the scripture (the promise), we are praying God's own words back to Him. God responds to His Word as it is truth. It is not based on how we feel. It is based on what we know to be true from Scripture.

2. How do you recognize God's voice when He speaks to you?

It will never contradict what God says in the Word.

3. How can you be sure it is God's voice and not your thoughts or the enemy's suggestions?

When God speaks to us, He speaks from our spirit, not our mind. The Bible tells us that our minds are enmity against God and are not subject to the law of God. Romans 8:7

It is that deep knowing inside — from our spirit — that we know it is God speaking to us.

4. Have you recognized God's voice? How did you respond?

Confirmation will always come from the Bible. God cannot say one thought from His Word and then something else from another source. If it is God speaking to you, His Word will confirm it.

Chapter 3
Understanding What Prayer Is

WE NEED TO understand what prayer is — how to pray scripturally and to fully realize we have been given that right. Prayer is joining forces with God the Father. It is fellowshipping with Him. God made the world, then He made man. God gave man dominion over all the work of His hands. But Adam committed high treason and sold out to Lucifer who then became the god of this world.

At that time, sin and death entered the world, and man lost his authority to the devil. But God had a plan of salvation for us and executed His plan by sending His Son Jesus to die for us. Jesus' death and resurrection did much more than just restore us to the same position Adam had; it placed us in a much higher position.

Ephesians 2:6 says: *"And raised us up together, and made us sit together in the heavenly places in Christ Jesus."*

And in Ephesians 1:20 – 23 *"Which He worked in Christ, when He raised Him from the dead, and seated Him at His own right hand in the heavenly places, far above all principality, and power, and might, and dominion, and every name that is named, not only in this age, but also in that which is to come: And He put all things under His feet and gave Him to be head over all things to the church, which is His body, the fullness of Him who fills all in all."*

Adam never held this position. Through Jesus' death and resurrection, we have received more than Adam had.

When we pray and understand the God-given authority we have, He will move on our behalf. The most important thing to grasp is how to pray according to God's design set in His Word. As we go through the steps you will discover how to pray in any given situation.

No set formulas guarantee if you pray a certain way one time the same blueprint will work the second time. This requires listening to your inner person, your spirit, where the Holy Spirit dwells. He will guide you.

Decide What You Need

When I prayed for Peter, I quoted the scripture that God will *give life to our mortal bodies.'* This is His promise. I did not pray for healing because Peter was almost dead and needed life only God could give.

Throughout the week following my visit with Peter, I reflected on what happened in that hospital room and prayed: "Thank you, Heavenly Father, for the opportunity to pray for Peter and for allowing me to be a part of this miracle."

Does that mean God would not have healed him if I had not been there? Perhaps. Does it mean I had to be the one who prayed? Maybe. But God always has a plan. God knows how we are going to respond when He asks us to do something. God knows how He is going to bless us when we step out of our comfort zone to do what He asks even when we face difficulties of our own.

The week after the miracle life spiraled downward for me. Clayton had been out of work for some time and his job search rendered no results, and we sank deeper into debt each day.

One dark, rainy November evening our twenty-year-old car stopped dead on the highway. I put the hood up, sat in my car, and wept. Nobody stopped to help. I felt so alone. Christmas was approaching, but we had no money to buy gifts for the kids. And no money to fix the car.

During my pity party, I sensed God's rebuke. Gently, yet firmly, He spoke to my heart, "If I can heal Peter, why would you entertain the thought I can't take care of you?"

Wow! That hit hard. Many times, we have faith when we pray for others but when it comes to our own lives, we fail miserably.

No phone. No flashlight. I had no choice but to walk in the blackness in search of a service station.

Rain poured, but I kept my pace over rocks and dirt. Finally, at the top of the exit ramp, I saw a gas station.

Nearly in tears and out of breath, I reached the station. "Can you please help me? My car broke down on the highway. I didn't run out of gas; it just stopped dead, but I managed to get it off the road and onto the shoulder."

The young attendant nodded and smiled at me, "Ma'am, I'll call a tow truck for you, but you'll have to be in your vehicle when it arrives."

If tears had fallen on my cheeks, they would have blended with the rain dripping from my hair. But I stayed calm and thanked him; walking down the hill would be easier and faster.

I arrived at my car chilled and frightened but then I remembered God's words to me. I didn't understand it but knew God was going to take care of me. He promises in Romans 8:28 that all things work together for our good. Not some things; but all things. I chose to trust that word and stay focused.

Clayton and I lived on a peninsula requiring a ferry trip to and from the city. The last ferry of the day was 9:30 PM. It was now 8:00 PM but God was fully aware of what time it was. He also knew I would not have any place to stay if I could not get home that evening. There was no way I could contact Clayton and he didn't know my dilemma.

"Heavenly Father, I know nothing surprised you tonight. I know you orchestrate my life. I know you love me and will take care of me. I choose to believe that everything will work out better than I could imagine. For these things I thank you."

Praying those words out loud in my car gave me the strength I needed.

The tow truck arrived, and I rode with the driver to the nearest full-service station. I expected the mechanic to have a solution, but he shrugged his shoulders.

"Sorry, Ma'am, we're about to close. I'll have someone look at it tomorrow."

"Tomorrow? Do you have any idea what the problem could be?" I pleaded for even a hint of reassurance.

"Sorry, I can't even guess until I have a look."

The tow truck driver asked me if I needed a lift to the ferry. "It's right on my way. I'd be happy to drive you there."

I wanted to hug him but instead, I signed relief and gave him a big smile. "Thank you."

I counted on God and knew He would also provide a way for me to get home from the ferry. I had less than twenty dollars in my purse which would only cover the cost of the ferry. Nothing would be left over to pay for a cab.

God knows exactly what is going to happen and is never shocked. He knows what we need but wants us to be precise when we make our requests. The more specific we are, the more we will appreciate the answer when it transpires.

"Thank you, Lord, for bringing me this far. I know you are with me, and you will provide a ride for me. And thank you for the promise that you will supply my needs." Ephesians 5:20 declares that I need to give thanks always, in all things.

The more I thanked Him, the more my joy built, moving me from a position of even the slightest doubt to one of unwavering faith. I was excited to see how God would arrange my transportation. There wasn't a chance He would ask me to walk thirty miles on a dark, wet, and cold night.

I sat in the cafeteria on the ferry wondering who I might recognize, knowing somehow God would have a ride available to get me home safely.

"Oh, my goodness. Is that you Carol?"

Swiftly I turned around.

"Tony! How good to see you. It's been at least a couple of years. Are you ready for Christmas?"

"Getting there. The kids are coming home this weekend which is why I went to the city today to get some last-minute shopping done. I'm so glad I ran into you because we moved to a house a few doors down the street from you and I have been meaning to stop by. You just saved me the trip."

Tony chuckled and gave me a warm hug.

I whispered, "Thank you, Jesus."

After sharing my broken-down car story with her, Tony offered to give me a lift. It gave us a great opportunity to catch up, and I was thrilled to rekindle a friendship. It was the end of an eventful, miracle-filled day.

I was exhausted when I arrived home after midnight but noticed the answering machine flashing. The message was from Peter's wife. I had not heard from anyone who was at the hospital since praying for Peter and didn't know if he was home yet.

"I want to thank you from the bottom of my heart for praying for Peter. The doctors said he would recover completely and there is no sign of cancer. This was truly a miracle."

I slowly sank to the floor, weeping, overcome with joy. "Thank you, God, for honoring Your Word. Nothing is too difficult for you. Absolutely nothing."

The next morning, I called the mechanic. "The timing chain is broken," he said, "and we will have to install a new one."

"What will that cost me?"

"Shouldn't run you more than a couple hundred dollars."

I wanted to shout, "I don't have a couple hundred dollars. I don't have twenty dollars." But instead, I thanked him and hung up.

I remembered God's words to me the day before and praised Him for supplying what I needed.

"Lord, I don't know where the money is going to come from. I don't know what to tell the mechanic. But I trust You and know You will provide."

Sometimes these words come easy and other times they can be a struggle. But I chose to believe God would provide. I chose to believe his Word which tells me all things work together for my good.

Within moments of that prayer of gratitude, the doorbell rang. I wondered if I should answer it.

What if it was a bill collector? What if they were here to turn off the electricity? "I know God is in control. I will not worry." I repeated this several times as I walked toward the door.

It was the mail carrier. He handed me a registered letter. My hands trembled slightly as I signed for it and wondered if we were being evicted.

I closed the door behind the mail carrier and slowly opened the letter.

Out loud I told myself, "Why are you allowing your fearful thoughts to grip you? Why do you immediately think of the worst-case scenario?"

I know it is common to have those thoughts. What makes the difference is what I do with them. Will I accept them and become fearful of impending doom? Or remind me that God knows the end of my story? He is in control. He will always find a way when there seems to be no way.

"Dear Clayton and Carol," the letter began. "Last week my wife and I were praying together, and God impressed upon each of us that He wanted us to bless you."

I was trying to remember who this couple was, but the memory was unclear.

"You may not remember us, but we met you about a year ago when we were visiting our daughter who lives in your town." I vaguely recalled.

"We hope you are not offended by this gift, but we felt strongly that God wanted us to send this to you. We hope you will be able to use it."

My mind stirred memories and then remembered which made me quiver when I read the next part of the letter.

"A few months ago, an acquaintance of ours called you and asked you to pray for a newborn baby who had just died. The doctors said there was no hope. He was gone. Even though that baby was already dead, you did not hesitate to speak life into that child."

I knew where this letter was headed. My heart beat fast and tears flowed freely down my cheeks.

"While you were praying for that child, he started to cough. God answered that prayer. Today he is a happy, healthy little boy."

I will never forget that phone call as I stood in awe of God's miracle power. I was ecstatic to hear the good news about the baby's health.

"When we were praying, God impressed on us to send this gift to you. We knew God had a reason. We are so happy to bless you for blessing others during their time of need."

I blinked. Then blinked again trying to clear my eyes as I gazed at the amount on the check -- $500. I looked again -- $5,000!

In the same way I prayed for Peter in the hospital, I had prayed for that baby. Standing on the promise in God's Word and not wavering in my faith when asking God to do what He promised is putting my faith and trust in His promise. Basing prayers on what God vowed to do when I dare to believe Him, is all He requires. He will perform the rest.

This was a lesson learned and not one I would soon forget. God orchestrates my life. His timing is perfect each time. He knows every intimate detail. God honors His Word. God only asks me to be obedient and to trust Him. That is all He asks of any of us.

1. Why should we be specific when we pray?
God knows what we need before we ask but when our requests are specific, we find the scripture to assure us we are praying God's will. His Word backs up our prayers and puts us in a position of authority.

2. Have you prayed the scripture for a specific need in your life?
Back your requests with the Word of God and thank God for His provision and favor in any situation.

3. If you are stressed, turn to scripture to find your answer.
Thank God for the answer. Then stand firm — God's timing is not your timing. "Let your requests be made known with thanksgiving in your heart" Philippians 4:6.

You have thanksgiving in your heart because you are resting in His promise.

Chapter 4
An Angel with a Message

CLAYTON WAS NINE months old when he was admitted to the hospital after being diagnosed with pneumonia. He improved quickly and was sent home a few days later.

However, the following week his parents became concerned that something was definitely wrong and that Clayton needed to go back to the hospital.

After two weeks in the hospital without any improvement, the doctors concurred that Clayton had contracted polio during his hospital stay. It affected the right side of his body, twisting his right arm behind his back and his right leg bent under the thigh of his left leg.

The doctor gave them this dreadful report. "I'm sorry, but there is nothing we can do. You need to prepare yourselves with the fact that Clayton will never walk or run. This is permanent. You will have to train him how to use one hand to do everything because he will never have the use of both arms."

"Why? How could this happen?" Clayton's father asked over and over again.

"There were children in the hospital with polio while Clayton was here," the doctor said. "Polio is highly contagious in the early stages. Precautions may not have been taken by the hospital staff. It happens."

Devastated, his parents had the medical staff's lame excuse along with the empty hope for Clayton's cure.

Clayton's dad was a pastor and early the next day he was at the church shoveling coal into the furnace for Sunday morning service.

He dropped to his knees and began to cry. "Why, God? I don't understand. Why?"

Almost immediately, he felt a calming presence. An angel appeared in front of him and said, "Do not worry about Clayton. He is going to be okay." That was it. The angel was gone in a flash. Mixed emotions rumbled in Clayton's dad including joy and bewilderment. He knew what he saw and heard. When would this miracle take place?

As he headed across the property to their house, Clayton's mother ran toward him. She had not taken the time to put on her coat. With tears running down her cheeks and her hands raised toward heaven, she yelled, "Clayton is healed! Clayton's healed!"

As she neared her husband she said, "Come quickly. You have to see this."

The two of them rushed into the nursery and she handed Clayton the bottle of milk. He immediately reached out with both hands to grab it. The withered side of his body had become straight without any sign of crippling.

They praised God together and this was only the first of many miracles in Clayton's life.

In this chapter, I will relate some of these truly astonishing stories of when angels protected Clayton or me. They taught us that God is always with us. He sends His angels not only to protect us but also to warn us.

Held in Mid-air by Unseen Angels

As a teenager, Clayton and his buddies often sped down the steep hills of his hometown on motorcycles.

But this time, when Clayton hit his brakes to slow down as he approached the red light, nothing happened. No brakes.

"Stop the traffic!" he screamed in terror, as he was flying towards the intersection. Immediately his friends realized what was wrong and they shrieked and swung their arms trying to slow down traffic.

It was too late. Clayton quickly realized his only two choices. He could go through the red light or try to negotiate a right turn straight into traffic. He chose to turn right. As he did, he hit a car head-on going 40 miles per hour.

Clayton was shot straight up and mysteriously stopped in mid-air. Unseen hands held him far above the accident below. He looked down and saw that traffic had come to a halt. Everyone was looking up and pointing. No one could believe what they saw. High above them, Clayton smiled at his friends as the angel set him down gently on the pavement.

He approached the driver of the car that hit him. "Are you okay, sir? I am so sorry, but my bike lost its brakes, and I couldn't stop."

The man could barely speak from the shock of what he just witnessed. He nodded indicating that he was fine.

Many people witnessed this accident. None could dispute they had observed a miraculous phenomenon. We will never know what lasting impact it made on their lives. But we can be sure God had a plan.

Psalms 91:11-12 tells us *"For He shall give His angels charge over you, to keep you in all your ways. In their hands, they shall bear you up, lest you dash your foot against a stone."*

I Saw My Guardian Angels

I drove down a country road in my brand-new pickup truck on a bright sunny day. Not only was it great to drive a new vehicle, but I felt safer than I did when I drove my last clunker.

Without warning, the steering wheel locked. I lost control and in a matter of seconds, the truck was in the ditch and flipped over. I was knocked unconscious and thrown several feet from the vehicle. This was before mandatory seatbelts, and I wasn't wearing one.

No one saw what happened. No traffic around. No homes anywhere. When I regained consciousness, I was on my back.

As I opened my eyes, two angels stepped away from me. They waved and smiled. Then they disappeared.

"Did I see them? Am I dreaming? How did I get out of the ditch?" Although I asked the questions out loud, no one was there to hear me.

"Thank you, Jesus, for protecting me but why did you send angels?"

I recognized that still, small voice who responded, "I want you to realize that I will always protect you. I will never leave you nor forsake you. I give angels charge over you."

Once again, God's promise of protection was fulfilled. Psalms 46:10 tells us *that God is our refuge and strength; a very present help in trouble.* In prayer, always remember to thank God for His protection. I am convinced that there are multiple times when God sends His guardian angels to protect us, even if we are not aware of it. Someday we may know the extent of that promise.

When God Answers an Old Question

Years later, when Clayton was praying, God reminded him of a time when an angel had protected him from certain death.

The summer Clayton turned 11, he helped his father close the summer cabin in preparation for winter. They needed to transport and store their Jeep at a friend's farm for the season.

"Help me hook up this long chain to the front of the Jeep," his dad instructed. "You can steer it while I pull it using my car."

When they stopped for gas Clayton stepped into the store. He decided how much of his allowance to spend on candy.

A voice said, "Spend it all. You won't be able to spend any for a long time."

Clayton spun around to see where the voice came from but there was no one else in the store.

The voice continued. "There is going to be a car accident, but you are going to be okay."

Fear gripped Clayton's young heart and he knew he couldn't say anything to his dad, who demanded his sons be tough. His dad would not be proud of him if he displayed notions of being a sissy.

When he got back to the Jeep, he gathered all the pillows and blankets from the backseat and piled them next to him — just in case. He thought he could dive under them if there was an accident.

Clayton relaxed after several miles as everything seemed to go smoothly until his dad turned onto a gravel road. Up ahead, a grader leveled two ridges of piled-up gravel. To pass the grader, the jeep had to cross over the ridges.

Clayton tried his best to steer the Jeep over the two-foot-high ridges, but the Jeep began to sway out of his control. The chain snapped. Clayton was thrown out of the driver's window into a nearly eight-foot-deep ditch. The Jeep's entire weight landed on top of him.

His dad watched as that vehicle defied all laws of physics. When the Jeep landed on Clayton it should have rested there. Instead, it seemed to have been picked up and thrown. It bounced out of the ditch nearly ten feet into the air, over a four-foot fence, and landed in the field on all four wheels.

Dad ran towards Clayton who sat in the ditch. Several of his teeth had been knocked out but amazingly he had only suffered some scrapes and bruises, no broken bones.

They both walked toward the Jeep. As they grew closer, shock filled them as they observed the details. His father pointed toward the vehicle. "Clayton, this is odd. Look how large the dent is in the roof of the Jeep where it landed on top of you, he said, "It's just not possible that your body could have made that large of an impression."

Years later, during prayer, the Lord reminded Clayton of how He had protected him. *"Your guardian angel laid on top of the Jeep and took the brunt of the impact."* Could that same angel have thrown the Jeep up into the air?

There are many mysteries we will never understand until eternity. But we can share how God protected us during those experiences. They serve as a reminder and a testimony of His promise from Psalms 91.

God protects us as He promised in His Word in numerous references. We do not need to fear but trust Him for the shelter He provides.

The Laws of Physics Defied — Again!

Enormous logging trucks traveling on the narrow two-lane highway were a usual occurrence. And as I encountered them during my daily drive, the tension increased when they approached from the opposite direction, particularly on a curve. I always took extra precautions gripping the steering wheel a bit tighter as I neared each bend.

Without warning, two of the four immense front tires from a logging truck speeded toward me. They approached my vehicle at a horrendous speed.

My heart pounded. "No!" I shouted out loud. "God help me!"

The rumble became deafening as they gained speed like steamrollers heading toward my car. Even if I wanted to, I couldn't swerve out of the way on that narrow road. I cried out loud again, "Help me, Jesus!"

As I watched those tires race towards my vehicle, the scenario seemed to be in slow motion but was only a split second. The tires separated right in front of me. They passed by either side of my car. I could hear the "whoosh" as they flew past my window.

I slowed down and pulled over when it was safe. The driver of the logging rig stopped in the middle of the highway, jumped out, and ran toward me.

I leaned my head out of the window and shouted at him, "Are you okay?"

His eyes were wide open. "Did you see that? I couldn't believe it. I ain't never seen nothin' like it in all my years as a trucker," his voice trembled, "I've seen some bad accidents when a semi loses a tire. But I lost two and they were headed right at you."

I nodded.

"Lady, you got angels around you or what?"

I burst into laughter in relief. I looked at him. "Yes, sir, I do. They always protect me."

He wiped his brow and inhaled a deep breath.

I smiled in understanding. "Do you want me to drive into town and send a tow truck to help you?"

"I'll be fine," he shook his head, "I'll radio for help but thanks. Ain't seen nothin' like it."

I smiled and waved. "I'll never forget this, and I'll pray for you whenever I think about it."

Just like any other promise in God's Word, He cannot lie. When we receive the truths and promises that are written and know in our hearts that God will perform what He has promised, then we can sleep well. We understand that God knows what we need before we even ask. How could we possibly know about impending danger? God does.

In Matthew 6:7 – 8, it says: *"And when you pray, do not use vain repetitions as the heathen do. For they think that they will be heard for their many words. Therefore, do not be like them. For your Father knows the things you have need of before you ask Him."*

None of these stories surprised God. He knew each circumstance beforehand and sent His angels to protect us. When we approach God with a thankful heart and believe that He has us in His hand, we do not have to live in fear.

Stories about angels may have been dismissed as 'fairy tales' but not anymore. There is no space in this book on miracles to cover the subject of angels.

New Age books teach about unscriptural and occultic angelic visitations of angels. I recommend Terry Law's book, *Truth About Angels: Encounters from a Biblical Perspective* if this subject interests you.

Terry Law reveals the truth about angels and how they are involved in the lives of believers. He shares numerous true stories from around the world that are undisputed.

Angels are prevalent in New Age teachings, but the Word tells us in 1 John 4:1 *"Beloved, do not believe every spirit but test the spirits to see whether they are of God."*

Terry Law's book clearly defines the angelic realm of Satan's angels and the role of God's angels. Any angelic message must line up with scripture and this book is an excellent study that teaches how to distinguish the difference between angels of light and angels of God. I Corinthians 11:14 says *Even Satan disguises himself as an angel of light.*

We are not to seek after angels or worship them. Terry Law addresses any questions you may have about angels in his book. It is thorough and based solely on the Word of God with numerous references.

1. If you have an encounter with an angel, how do you test it to be sure it is from God?

"Beloved, do not believe every spirit but test the spirits to see whether they are of God" 1 John 4:1.

We are warned in 2 Corinthians 11:14, "Even Satan disguises himself as an angel of light."

Did the angelic being tell you that it has appeared because you are a chosen person from a special group of evolved humans?

Did he encourage you to pray to it or to worship it?

Did he promise to reward you with material wealth in exchange for your devotion?

Various scriptures advise us that angels are not to be worshiped, and true heavenly beings will discourage humans who attempt to bow down to them.

"By this, you know the Spirit of God: Every spirit that confesses that Jesus Christ has come in the flesh is of God, and every spirit that does not confess that Jesus Christ has come in the flesh is not of God. And this is the spirit of the antichrist, which you have heard was coming and is now already in the world" 1 John 4:2 – 4.

Chapter 5
Understanding Our Authority

IT WAS AFTER midnight when my husband, Clayton opened the sliding glass door to let our cat outside. He noticed a pair of eyes illuminated by the porch light and stepped onto the deck to get a closer look across the 100-foot yard. Before he took the second step, a large mountain lion lunged toward him from across the lawn.

No time to think. No time to turn around. Boldness gripped Clayton as he leaned toward the approaching mountain lion who was in midair. He could feel that monster's breath and he shouted, "In the Name..." Without a second hesitation, the cougar twisted its body to retreat as his tail brushed Clayton's face.

When Clayton came back inside, I noticed his hand was shaking. "What happened to you?"

"A mountain lion tried to attack me, but God stopped it in midair." My mouth dropped open and I gasped. "How can that happen so fast? You were out there for only a minute!" I drew my conclusion. Of course, God protected him from all harm.

Clayton said "The verse in Luke 10:19 flashed before my eyes, which says God gives us the power to tread on serpents and scorpions and all the power of the enemy. But I didn't have time to say anything except 'in the Name.'"

Clayton fully grasped the authority we have in Christ. Fear had no legal territory there. When we dare to believe that God's Word is true, we can stand on it without any doubt.

"I was attacked by a huge mountain lion last night," Clayton told the local Conservation Officer the next morning.

"We're aware that there's one in this area but haven't been able to trap it. According to the sightings, he's the largest local one on record. He must be around 300 pounds. How close did he get to you?"

Clayton didn't hesitate. "The cat had already glided over the porch railing and was within inches of my face."

"And he didn't attack you?" The officer raised his eyebrows in disbelief.

"I could feel his breath on my face as he did a 180 and ran away." Clayton was reliving the moment.

"We keep a leather dog collar hanging on a hook by our door. I found it in our yard this morning and noticed it had been chewed. This mountain lion must have been starving."

"Well, my friend, you have witnessed a miracle. This creature is out for blood. He's hungry and ruthless. You're one lucky man."

Lucky? I don't think so. Luck had nothing to do with it. Understanding and knowing how to apply God's promise of protection was evident.

A few days later, with a slight chuckle in his voice, the officer confirmed they had captured the lion and transported him many miles away. "In my years on the force, I have never heard of one retreating. He is the largest mountain lion on record, and I can't believe he didn't have you for lunch."

No matter what may attempt to attack us, we have nothing to fear. We have a God-given authority over any assault. That authority promises us "Greater is He that is in you than he that is in the world" I John 4:4.

The definition of authority is the power or right to give orders, make decisions, and enforce obedience. That lion had no option but to obey Clayton. God had given Clayton authority when he chose to believe he had it.

If we allow it, fear can be a controlling factor in our lives. Franklin D. Roosevelt said, "There is nothing to fear but fear itself."

He went on to say: "Fear is a nameless, unreasoning, unjustified terror which paralyzes needed efforts to convert retreat into advance." The absence of fear makes us advance, not run in terror.

When doubt tries to steal the promise, we have the authority to use scripture — our greatest weapon against doubt or fear.

If asked this question, how would you answer? "Do you honestly believe God would protect you if a lion attacked you?"

Thinking about that scenario may cause you to shudder but understanding the promise God gives us is our defense. There is a multitude of scriptures assuring us we have nothing to fear. Meditating on these by engraining them into our psyche will give us the strength and boldness we need when faced with a roaring lion. Then we will have the foundation to draw from when we need it.

It is our instinct to imagine the worst. The what-ifs can bring worry that has no real foundation. But if we consistently replace those thoughts with the promise of protection, soundness of mind, and the power given to us through Christ, those thoughts will dissipate as promised in II Timothy 1:7.

That power God has given us applies not only to danger, or crisis but to a medical diagnosis that could bring us to fear.

Receiving the diagnosis of terminal cancer when I was a young woman could have destroyed my world. Instead, I stood up, faced it head-on, and told the doctor God's truth, "I will walk in here pregnant one day."

Did I have confirmation of that? Did I have access to future events? A resounding "No." What I did have was God's promise which cannot lie. My faith responded — not my fear. How He chose to work out the details was not my concern. God's facts overrule man's reports.

Fear robs us. Peace empowers us.

Fear can destroy us. The truth of God's Word restores us.

Fear is a robber of rational thoughts. But we have a weapon of mass destruction when we use the Word against negativity in our thought realm.

The only weapon Jesus used in the wilderness to defeat the devil was the Word of God. *"But He answered and said, it is written, man shall not live by bread alone, but by every word that proceeds from the mouth of God"* Matthew 4:4.

Clayton had the Word in his heart. He knew he had nothing to fear when he approached that lion. That beast needed to fear Clayton and he did as he ran away defeated.

Jesus understood His authority. He knew that when He spoke the Word, it would come to pass. We have been given that same authority.

It is not a matter of memorizing scriptures. It is understanding that God's Word is true. He cannot lie. Our job is to believe that. When we grip the truth, we can rest in it.

1. How do we get bold in our faith?

When we understand who we are in Christ Jesus and that all the promises are ours, we will realize we have nothing to fear. If we confess how fearful we are in a situation, the fear will grow. If we confess the Word in the same situation, it builds our faith and gives us the boldness and stamina we need to stand firm.

2. If you encountered a mountain lion, would you be afraid or have the boldness you needed to make it turn and run? If not.....why not?

3. When you are in fear, what do you do? Do you need to change your response in these circumstances? What will you do differently next time?

Chapter 6

Pray the Answer — Not the Problem

MY DREAM TO someday be a mommy began as a little girl. In my twenties, the ovarian cancer diagnosis not only shattered that dream but threatened my life as well. I needed God's healing — for me and my husband. And yes, I needed a child.

Finding scriptures that promised healing was easy. I wrote them down. I read them out loud. I believed Joshua 1:8 which says I must speak the Word, meditate on it day and night, and believe it.

Our prayers need to be a statement of faith instead of unbelief, which is simply praying the answer instead of the problem. They need to fall into line with that truth, not with the circumstances around us or the lies we could so easily believe. We need to choose to stand on God's Word that He has healed us. He knows what we need. His Word is true, and we should count on His healing power instead of questioning if He will perform what He has promised.

Many scriptures, including Isaiah 53:5, confirm our healing was finalized on the cross. *"But He was wounded for our transgressions, He was bruised for our iniquities; the chastisement for our peace was upon Him, and by His stripes, we are healed."*

At times it may be difficult to understand, but we must realize it is God's timing — not ours. The battle which ensues can be a struggle unless we learn how to win that fight through prayer.

Let your prayers be with gratitude. "Heavenly Father, you know the future. You knew the end of my story before I was aware of the problem. You promised to heal and restore me before I realized I was sick. I will focus on those promises and not on how I am feeling. You will do what You have promised and for that, I thank you."

According to Matthew 6:8, if God already knows what we need before we ask Him, why does He tell us to ask? The answer lies in Philippians 4:6 *"Be anxious for nothing, but in everything by prayer and supplication with thanksgiving let your requests be made known to God."*

Therein lies one of the greatest secrets to answered prayer. When we believe that God has promised what we need, He will supply. We will not be anxious or worried. We will pray a prayer of thanksgiving; thereby letting our petitions be made known to Him by thanking Him for the answer He has already provided.

Instead of begging God to intervene, we need to use scripture that applies to our needs and thank Him in advance for His provision.

The time between choosing to believe the promise of God's Word and the actual manifestation is undetermined. It could be instant, or it could delay, so much so it may seem like an eternity. This period is referred to as 'the trial of our faith.' 1 Peter 1:7 says: *"That the trial of your faith, being much more precious than of gold that perishes, though it be tried (tested) with fire, might be found unto praise and honor and glory at the appearing of Jesus Christ."*

Often, we feel like we are put through the fire with no end in sight. That trial, no matter how long it lasts, is precious to the Father. He is fully aware of what we are going through. He is pleased when we continue to believe Him despite negative circumstances. How easy it would be to say, "Forget it. It is never going to happen. God didn't hear my cry." Is there a point when we should stop believing or do we continue praying the promise, which is the answer?

James 1:6-8 says: *"But let him ask in faith, with no doubting, for he who doubts is like a wave of the sea driven and tossed by the wind. For let not that man think that he may receive anything from the Lord he is a double-minded man, unstable in all his ways."*

When our thoughts and our voice agree to speak faith, we turn our defeats into victory. We must make a concentrated effort not to accept defeat. Remember this is a battle. A trial of our faith. It is our God-given right to have what He has promised. It is ours. It will come. Accept it and watch it become a reality.

But as reality unfolds, we're tempted to question the timing of His answer or the way He's providing it to us. It is easy to say: "Well, I guess it wasn't God's will." We are subconsciously saying that God is a liar. "Even though He said it, obviously it was not for me." God is not a respecter of persons. His Word is for every believer. *"For there is no partiality with God"* Romans 2:11.

When we realize God does not play favorites and that His promises are for everyone, we can stand assured on God's facts. The answer He promised in His Word is already accomplished. He has already moved on our behalf when He gave up Jesus to die for us. However, when we confess His Word, it moves us from a position of doubt to faith. It moves our hearts from a position of "Is it true?" to "I believe it!" Joshua 1:8 tells us that when we meditate on His Word, we will make our way prosperous, and then we will have success.

Sadly, sometimes it is easier to believe the lies that scream at us than to believe the truth God gives us. Then we conjure up reasons why our prayers may not be answered.

You may ask yourself, "How do you know it is God's will to heal you? What if He has other plans?"

"What if God wants to keep me humble by keeping me poor?"

"How can I know God has forgiven my past?"

Realize deeply that God never has a different plan or opinion. If He promised to heal in His Word, it is a promise we can bank on. If His Word declares prosperity, we have the right to believe in it. He does not change his mind. His will is His Word. Period.

Satan also is consistent in his efforts. Doubt is one of the tools he loves to use against us. If he can make us doubt, he has his foot in the door. We may start questioning our faith.

Instead of questioning, we pray the promises which is praying God's will. When we have the Word in our hearts, our prayers will be in line with the Word. We do not need to worry if it is God's will. His will is clearly stated in His Word. This is the only way to have a successful prayer life. The understanding of the Word must be first and foremost.

The Bible tells us to fight the good fight of faith. (I Timothy 6:12) In the natural, if someone were trying to rob you and take your home away from you, what would you do? You would fight for it with everything in your power.

Yet, when it comes to spiritual things and we are confronted with conflict, we often roll over and play dead. If God's Word says that we have certain things, then they belong to us. If the enemy, or our negative thinking, tells us differently, we need to fight those thoughts.

When Jesus was tempted by Satan in the wilderness, his response was to quote the Word which defeated the enemy each time.

We must eliminate any image, suggestion, or feeling that does not contribute to God's truth. Those destructive thoughts are planted as seeds. If we nurture them, they will grow. If we ignore them, they will fade and die. This trial of our faith may not be easy but worth every bit of effort and time it takes to witness the manifestation of God's promise.

As I lay on the sofa in intense pain, God revealed to me that my healing was already promised. My job was to believe it. To thank Him for it. To stand strong in my belief and ward off doubt and fear by quoting the promise. The Bible promises that "Blessed is she who believed, for there will be a fulfillment of those things which were told her from the Lord" Luke 1:45. The more I quoted the promise the more I believed it and the more excited I became.

While I waited 14 years to become pregnant, I could have stopped believing the promise at any time. I could have stopped at 13 years or one year. Would that have made a difference? Most definitely. Was I willing to take that chance? Never. Did I ask God why it was taking so long? No. I did not have to. That was not my job. My contract with God was a signed one. He promised. I believed. He signed it with the blood of His Son, Jesus. There was no room for doubt. God's timing is perfect. Every. Time.

God made the promise, and He is a God of His Word. I hung on. The more I proclaimed and thanked God for my healing the more excited I became. I did not doubt it. I chose to believe it. I did not question why it was taking so long. That was in God's timing. Whenever I felt discouraged, I would praise God for His promise and thank Him that He would fulfill that promise because it was declared as His will.

1. **Do you recall any time you prayed the answer? Did you waver or stand firm?**

When we pray the scriptures and the promises, we can rest assured God hears and He answers. Every. Time. We do not know His timing. Our responsibility is not to guess what God's timing is but to trust Him that He knows exactly what He is doing and be confident He is responding.

2. How many times did you get an instant answer?

3. How often did you have to wait? Was it difficult? How did you increase your faith to remain steadfast?

4. If you do not get the answer in 'due' time, do you automatically think that it is not God's will?

5. How do you control your doubts when you see other people get answers and you struggle with waiting on God?

Chapter 7
How to Understand God's Will

WHEN JESUS PRAYED, He never said if it is Your will. At Lazarus' tomb, He did not say "If it is thy will." What He did say was "Father, I thank You that You have heard Me. And I know that You always hear Me, but because of the people who are standing by I said this, that they may believe that You sent Me."

"Now when He had said these things, He cried with a loud voice, "Lazarus, come forth!" And he who had died came out bound hand and foot with graveclothes, and his face was wrapped with a cloth. Jesus said to them, *"Loose him and let him go"* John 11: 41 – 44.

When Jesus, in the most extreme circumstance, showed us the solution is "Father, I thank You." How much more should we thank God in the middle of any problem we face? If the prayer of thanksgiving can raise the dead, then we need to give thanks despite any negative circumstances and we will see victory. When we pray the prayer to change circumstances, never put an 'if' in front of it. Stand firm on the promise God gave you.

We will never comprehend what Jesus went through when He was about to die. He cried out to His Father, "Father, if it is Your will, take this cup away from Me; nevertheless, not My will, but Yours, be done." This is the only time Jesus asked God if it was His will as He knew his demise. It is not a pattern for prayer as it is an isolated instance.

45

When we think of our Savior's death, we grieve knowing the horrific physical suffering He endured in our place. However, we must also realize how He must have agonized mentally and emotionally. His heart broke for us.

Scientists tell us that after a severely stressful situation, we can have an adrenaline rush unlike any other. The left ventricle of the heart takes on a cone-like shape that resembles the shape of a pot the Japanese use to capture octopuses called 'tako-tsubo" which means "fishing pot for trapping octopus." Tako-tsubo Cardiomyopathy is now Broken Heart Syndrome's medical name.

Wikipedia defines it as a sudden temporary weakening of the myocardium (the muscle of the heart). This weakening can be triggered by severe emotional stress. Stress cardiomyopathy is a well-recognized cause of acute heart failure.

Like Jesus, when someone is flogged, they often go into hypovolemic shock, a term that refers to low blood volume. There is evidence from Scripture that Jesus experienced a hypovolemic shock because of being beaten thirty-nine times for our healing.

Before death, the sustained rapid heartbeat caused by hypovolemic shock also causes fluid to gather in the sack around the heart and lungs. This gathering of fluid in the membrane around the heart is called pericardial effusion, and the fluid gathering around the lungs is called pleural effusion. This explains why, after Jesus died and a Roman soldier thrust a spear through His side, piercing both the lungs and the heart, blood and water poured out just as John explained in John 19:34.

When I realized how much Jesus suffered not only physically but mentally and emotionally, I understood how he could have undoubtedly died of a broken heart.

There have been times in my life when I did not know if I could put one foot in front of the other and continue living. The heartache was intense. The agony seemed endless. But as hopeless as each situation appeared, I praised God for making me a victor instead of a victim; for giving me His promises, and for assuring me that He was in control.

During one of these times God spoke directly to my heart and said, "Carol, because I suffered from a broken heart, I understand your pain. I took all the sin, all the guilt, all the condemnation upon myself on the cross. I experienced that agony on your behalf."

If we do something we should not do and feel guilty, we feel terrible. Now, imagine Jesus taking on all our sins and all our guilt; carrying the weight of that burden so we don't have to. Multiply that by billions of times for each person he died for.

When we grasp the extent of what Jesus went through emotionally, we understand why He needed to go through heartbreak to relate to our sorrow. This is why we can praise Him no matter what we are going through. He knows. He understands — in every respect.

If we whine or complain about our circumstances, they tend to magnify and all we see is the problem. Thanksgiving is the language of faith that pleases God. We are not thanking God for the problems but for the answers He has already provided in His Word.

Our prayer should be: "Thank you, Heavenly Father, for providing the answer to my situation in your Word. I stand on your Word. I will not allow doubt to rob it. Your Word is truth. It is absolute. I choose to believe your Word and I thank you for that provision."

When we need healing, we know God's Word is clear. We stand on the scriptures that God's will is for us to be healthy and prosperous — even as our soul prospers. *"Beloved, I pray that you may prosper in all things and be in health, just as your soul prospers"* 3 John:2.

Proverbs 4:20 - 22 tells us *"Give attention to my words; incline your ear to my sayings. Do not let them from your eyes; keep them in the midst of your heart. For they are life to those who find them, and health to all their flesh."* It could not be any clearer. God's Word is health to our flesh. When we pray the answer that is already in the Bible and refuse to doubt, we will see the manifestation of that promise for our needs. It is not hoping, it is believing.

Have you ever heard the expression 'hope and pray?' Are you hoping God will heal you? Are you hoping a difficult situation will turn around? The Bible gives us promises. When we pray the promise, we are praying God's words back to Him. We are thanking Him that His Word is true. He cannot lie.

When we are aware that the answer to our situation is already promised in the Word of God, it is easy to pray that promise, believe that promise, and thank God for His promise. There is an enormous difference between hoping and praying or praying and knowing.

We do not necessarily pray about many things in our life that occur daily such as:

"I hope it doesn't rain tomorrow."

"I hope I get there on time in this traffic."

These are normal things we hope for. But when we say we are hoping and praying, we are contradicting the Word. If we have prayed in faith for healing, then we do not have to hope God heard us or that He will answer. He has already established His will regarding our healing in His Word. Our job is to believe it, not waver in our faith, and thank Him for answering our prayers.

Praying the answer instead of the problem puts us in a position of belief. We are praying God's Word back to Him, thanking Him for that answer. It builds our faith and brings us to a place of assurance instead of doubt.

1. When your heart is breaking and you cannot see a solution to your pain, what do you do?

2. Do you use the expression 'hope and pray'?

3. Do you understand the difference between hoping and praying?

Chapter 8

The Power in the Prayer of Agreement

"MOM, THERE HAS been a terrible accident. Please pray. Amy might not make it."

My son Jason's voice was high-pitched and awakened me out of deep sleep early that morning.

The night before I hosted a bridal shower for Sara, my daughter-in-law to be. Amy, Sara's sister, and Maid of Honor left the party early. I feared it was because of a conversation I overheard that she needed to make a connection for drugs. I knew she struggled with addiction. This phone call conjured up terrible thoughts of what might have happened.

"What? Oh, no! What happened?"

"The medivac flew her to the nearest trauma center and Sara and I are headed there now."

Even though it would take several hours for me to get to the hospital, I knew I had to leave. Now.

"Jason, I will get there as soon as possible."

"Please don't come, Mom."

As long as I had known Sara, she vocalized she wanted nothing to do with God. Although this grieved my heart, Jason's life was in God's hands and a meddling mom would not change his mind in his decision to marry someone against his Christian upbringing.

So, I embraced Sara in every way I could. Her mother had abandoned her when she was twelve and Sara had never been shown love as a teenager. I often took her shopping and poured kindness into her life. In recent years Sara and her mom had built a new relationship but she had missed so much as a teenager.

Before Sara and Jason were married, I asked her if it would be okay for me to give her a bridal shower. Her response was "Okay with me? Are you kidding? I didn't think I would have a shower. Can I help you plan it?"

The shower was a big hit, and a new bond was formed between Sara and me. But we never talked about God. The timing wasn't right.

I understood why Jason asked me not to come to the hospital. "Mom, you know Sara's family is anti-God and they wouldn't want you in there praying."

Although I did not fully understand why God wanted me at that hospital, I did believe that He was about to perform a miracle.

"Don't worry, Jason. I'm not going to cause a scene or do anything to embarrass you."

I arrived at the hospital around noon and located Sara's mom, Vickie, in the ICU waiting room. Her glare made me shiver. I felt like an intruder and needed to be exceptionally careful about how I approached her.

"Vickie, I am so sorry. You must be worried. Can you share what happened?"

"Amy's car spun out of control on a curve late last night. She was thrown from the car and landed upside down in the ditch. She had been knocked unconscious and no one noticed the car until five o'clock this morning."

"What are the doctors saying? Is she going to be okay?"

Her voice cracked. "No, there is little hope. I'm waiting for the next update, but it doesn't look good."

I suppressed my desire to grab her and hold her close, everything in me wanted to shout my excitement at the impending miracle. But I kept my distance and remained calm. Vickie needed her privacy.

Earlier when I left our house, Clayton and I agreed in prayer that God would restore Amy. Clayton said he would intercede until he felt a breakthrough. Therefore, there was no doubt in my mind that God would perform a miracle.

"I need to go to the restroom," Vickie announced, possibly as a means of escape. I took the opportunity to call Clayton.

"It is much worse than we thought, Clayton."

Clayton spoke firmly. "About a half-hour ago God spoke clearly to my heart that Amy will be fully restored. So, let that be confirmation to you."

"I agree and felt that as I drove down here."

I glanced down the hallway, my stomach tightening as a loud guttural groan echoed throughout. A doctor held Vickie to keep her from collapsing.

I wanted to run to her but stood still. I yearned to shout that God was in control and He was about to perform a miracle. I kept silent.

When the doctor left, I slowly approached Vickie and hugged her. Her body stiffened. Then I asked her what the doctor said.

"She's gone, Carol. Amy's spine was broken in several places. There was severe brain trauma and even if she survived the physical injuries she would be in a coma for the rest of her life. Nothing can change that — there is no hope. None."

"Vickie, I died when I was a baby and my dad's prayer brought me back to life. I believe in miracles and know several people who were never supposed to live, and they are alive today."

"God loves you and your daughters. He longs for a relationship with you and to show you how much He loves and cares about you. He wants Amy to be completely healed and if you allow me to, I would like to pray with you."

Tears streamed down her cheeks as she slightly nodded in agreement. "But it won't do any good. The doctor is removing her life support. He asked that I sign the papers at 2:30 this afternoon."

"Thank you, heavenly Father," I began as I took her hands in mine, "that you love each of us so much. Thank you for creating Amy. Because you created her, I know you can fix her. Thank you for allowing me to be here today to show Vickie how much you love her. Thank you for the miracle we are about to witness."

I felt her hands relax. She smiled slightly at me as I said goodbye.

"Please have Jason call me later. Rest assured you are going to get a good report."

I left.

I quivered.

A terrible voice was screaming at me. "The whole family is going to laugh at you when she dies. You should have stayed home."

I rebuked the thought, but it was nagging and desperately trying to create doubt.

On the long drive home, I wept as I thanked God for his mercy. I thanked Him I could be part of this phenomenon only He could perform.

As I approached the ferry my phone rang. I glanced at the time. It was 2:30.

"MOM!" Jason was shouting.

"You're not going to believe this. Fifteen minutes ago, Amy opened her eyes, sat straight up in bed, and asked for coffee and chocolate. The nurse almost fainted because she was in the room preparing to pull the plug."

I laughed out loud with a joy that burst within me. "Thank God."

"Amy told the nurse she wanted to get out of bed but was reminded she couldn't walk. Can you believe it, Mom?"

"Did Amy remember the accident?"

"No, and she couldn't believe she almost died."

During the next few weeks, Amy required some physical therapy, but she was able to attend Jason's wedding and walked down the aisle as Maid of Honor.

When I prayed with Vickie it was a simple prayer she needed to hear. But the prayer that brought this victory was the prayer of agreement Clayton and I shared before I left my house.

Matthew 18:19 says *"Again, I say to you that if two of you shall agree on earth concerning anything that they ask, it will be done for them by My Father in heaven."*

Notice the word 'shall' in verse 19. The strongest assertion we can make in the English language is to say, "I shall" or "I will." In the original Greek, it translates, *"If you shall ask anything in my name, and I don't have it, then I will make it for you."*

There was no doubt that God's will was for Amy to survive and be a testimony of God's power and grace. During those hours of travel to the hospital, Clayton and I continued to pray the scriptures and thanked God for the miracle.

When I prayed with Vickie at the hospital, I already knew God would restore Amy. Doubt fled. Rejoicing before the manifestation was effortless.

We may pray to ask God to please do something about a situation instead of believing with our hearts and saying it with our mouths. When we realize God already has done something about it and has given us the promise we need in any situation, it is easy to exercise our faith. When two of us agree together it is that much more powerful.

The Bible says that "...one will put one thousand to flight (referring to demons), but two will put ten thousand to flight." Deuteronomy 32:30 and Leviticus 26:8. There is immense power in agreeing in prayer with another believer.

When Clayton and I agreed in prayer it was like a boost of faith. We also prayed the scriptures that gave us the authority for the prayer of agreement.

1. Have you ever prayed the prayer of agreement? Did you sense the strength in numbers?

2. If you have any doubts when you pray, do you find it helpful to ask someone to agree with you?

Chapter 9
The Prayer that Unlocks Heaven

ON A BRISK Spring morning, I headed home from an eight-day speaking tour in southern Washington and paced myself to avoid rush-hour traffic. I stopped for breakfast outside of Seattle and called my husband.

"Good morning, honey. I'm on schedule and should be able to meet up with you later this afternoon. It's a gorgeous day and I can't wait to get home."

"Drive carefully. There are always idiots on the freeways."

"You know I will."

Although both of us tended to be speeders, we always made sure to be alert to the traffic around us.

Interstate 5 is a five-lane highway with a speed limit of 70 mph. While in the center lane, I noticed a police officer on a motorcycle two car lengths in front of me. I glanced at my speedometer to be sure I kept to the speed limit.

Suddenly a black car edged too close to my right, traveling at the same speed. My body tensed as I noticed our side-view mirrors were about an inch apart. Without time to check my rear-view mirror, I moved over to the next lane, and she followed, just as close. I pressed down on my horn, but she didn't respond. I eased off the accelerator to slow down and what happened next became a blur.

My hands gripped the wheel tightly; my heart beat fast and my body shook. With everything in me, I shouted, "Jesus!"

There was no time for me to react or apply the brakes. Her car crashed against the cement meridian and spun sideways. My SUV headed directly to her front door.

Here is where all laws of physics were defied.

I did not apply the brakes but my truck stopped immediately, within inches of her door.

Nothing was tossed inside my vehicle. My speed was between 65 and 68 mph. The engine did not die. The stop was strangely gentle as if I were traveling at 10 mph, not 65.

As her airbag deployed, she held her cell in her right hand. Had she been texting at that speed? Was she trying to kill herself?

Traffic slowed and a couple of drivers pulled up to see if we were okay. I took a deep breath of relief yet felt overwhelmed with disbelief. I noticed that I was trembling.

The front of the girl's car was completely fragmented and gone. A man asked me to back up my truck to give him room to open her door and pull her out.

Then he came back to report, "She said it was a rental car (brand new) and the steering was wonky."

The steering was wonky? Not so. Why was she going at that speed? And why didn't she attempt to stop?

Then he asked a question that baffled me. "What's this in front of your car?"

No answers. Only the undeniable fact that a pile of sand stopped my truck gently, without incident.

I looked at him. "My angels put it there!"

He gave a crooked smile and shook his head in disbelief.

There is only one explanation for what happened: divine intervention. There is no doubt, nor any rationalization. Truly, it was a miracle.

When I called out the name of Jesus it was with the assurance He was with me and would protect me. Even in that split second, faith overcame fear.

As I continued my trip home, God overwhelmed me with His peace and the experience reminded me of a small child playing with a toy car. The child holds a car in his hand making the wheels go faster and faster and then places it on the floor. It doesn't move. The one who held it in his hand — stopped it.

To comprehend the impact of using the name of Jesus, we need to understand our authority.

Jesus has given us the power of attorney to use His name. His name has all authority on earth, and we are permitted to use it. Without that understanding, we may struggle in the thought arena and feel whipped by the enemy. When we understand our power, we are in the arena of faith and the devil is the victim, not us.

When we walk as victors instead of victims, we are in charge. It is common to run to a church leader to ask for a 'powerful' prayer. But we have the right to pray that powerful prayer with authority and anointing. We do not need to ask for it but thank God that He has given it to us.

Even in a moment of sheer terror, we can call on the name of Jesus for protection. The anointing is our authority, and the name is our weapon.

When I shouted the name of Jesus, I was fully aware of the power, authority, and protection that comes from that name. Instantly, I knew I was safe, and this would be a testimony.

When we are born again, the Holy Spirit comes to dwell in us, to live in our spirit. He never leaves us. We do not have to pray for the anointing because according to scripture we are anointed. Praying for the anointing is nullifying His presence.

The anointing gives us the power and authority to be victorious; whether it is a confrontation with a mountain lion or praying for someone who needs healing from God. When we pray the answer, we need to believe it. When we believe it, it empowers us. We know Who is behind the promise and we trust Him without reservation when we realize His anointing dwells in us: 100% of the time.

In II Corinthians 1:21, I John 2:20, and I John 2:27 we read that we are anointed and the anointing which we have received abides in us. When we pray to ask for the anointing, we are not believing what scripture has told us — that we are anointed by Christ dwelling in our spirit.

Just as the anointing is the authority, the name of Jesus is the weapon. We have a weapon of mass destruction when we understand the power of attorney we possess. Jesus gave us His name to use as a weapon. At the name of Jesus, every knee shall bow. His name is above every other name. It is above disease, pain, fear, and all things in heaven and earth.

Philippians 2:9 assures us that everything is subject to the name of Jesus; every knee shall bow, and every tongue confess that Jesus Christ is Lord.

No matter what type of situation we encounter, we need to be fully aware of the anointing within us. It gives us the authority to be in command. The anointing is the empowerment of authority.

1. **How do we know we have the God-given authority to pray and expect an answer?**

2. **How do we know we have the anointing? Do we need to pray and ask God for it? Why or why not?**

3. **Do you believe the scripture that tells us we will see greater works (miracles) than Jesus did during His time on earth? Why or why not?**

Chapter 10
Authority and Ammunition

ON A TWO-WEEK speaking tour in England, my husband Clayton welcomed a day of rest. It was the middle of February with gray skies and daily downpours; a day off gave him a respite from his travels across London.

"Not sure why," he told me later, "but early that morning I sensed an urge to fast and pray. I trusted God would reveal the reason why."

At four o'clock that afternoon, his phone rang. A young man introduced himself as someone who had been in one of the meetings.

"My name is Oliver. My mother, Lois, is in ICU at the Sherwood Forest Hospital. I am wondering if you would be willing to pray for her?"

Clayton asked, "Do you believe God can heal her?"

"Yes, I do, which is what prompted me to contact you." Clayton agreed to meet with Oliver at 7 PM which gave him time to ask God how to specifically pray in this situation.

But he did not receive any direction. Nothing. No inspiration.

As the two of them drove across the city, Oliver explained his mother's condition.

"My mom had surgery this week. When they opened her up and saw the extent of cancer in her esophagus, they stitched her back up and said she had three days to live if that."

"Three days to live?" Clayton thought. "What did I get myself into? I don't know how to specifically pray for this. Lord, you have not given me any clear direction."

The more Oliver talked; the more hopeless Clayton was feeling. He heard the desperation in Oliver's voice and knew God was able but the battle in his mind would not cease.

Clayton wanted to know how to pray effectively. He was depending on hearing from God to direct him and felt ill-equipped until he walked through the doors of the hospital.

Sometimes it feels like God is too late, but that is untrue.

As the doors opened the voice in Clayton's spirit resounded with clarity. "Take authority against the spirit of infirmity and the spirit of death."

That was it.

Clayton was acutely aware of the authority the Word gave him and the anointing that dwelled in his spirit. Now, God had given him the ammunition.

As he stepped into the intensive care unit, he saw a mere shell of a woman. She was emaciated. Her skin color was gray. Several tubes were giving her life support, but she was unconscious and lifeless.

Clayton stood at the foot of Lois' bed and spoke softly but firmly. "In the name of our Lord Jesus Christ, I take authority against the spirit of death and the spirit of infirmity that are trying to destroy this woman. You have no legal territory here and you must leave."

Oliver, his father, and his brother looked at Clayton in shock. "Is that it? Is that all you're going to pray?"

"Yes, that's what God told me to do."

Clayton glanced back at Lois and a tear was running down her cheek. He did not know if anything had changed but he knew he had been obedient. The tear made him realize that she heard the prayer.

A few days later Clayton flew back to the United States but had not heard any more from Oliver.

Although we are obedient when God asks us to pray for someone, there are times we never hear the results of our prayers. It is not unusual to want answers on our schedule, but we have to trust God to perform what He has promised.

In 2 Chronicles 20:12, it says, *"Do not be afraid nor dismayed because of this great multitude, for the battle is not yours, but God's."* We need to leave it there. We did our part. God fights the battle, and He never loses.

Months later Clayton received a phone call. "Hi. You don't know me, but we attended the conference you spoke at in London. We need to discuss something with you. Would you be able to meet us near the airport?"

Intrigued, we both met with them at a restaurant near the Vancouver airport.

"We were going to tell you this on the phone but felt it would be better to tell you in person. Besides, we wanted to see the look on your faces."

Their faces did not indicate if they had good news or if they needed prayer. But their demeanor changed as they began their story.

"Do you remember the lady whom you prayed for in London who was dying?"

"Yes, of course."

"The morning after you prayed for her, she woke up from her coma, sat up in bed, and asked for something to eat."

They both had huge smiles and enjoyed every second as they shared the details of this miracle.

"When Lois sat up in bed, pulling the tubes from her mouth, the attending nurse looked perturbed and was adamant. 'You may be hungry but remember, you can't swallow. Please lie back down and I will get someone to put the tube back into your mouth.'"

"I couldn't talk before, but I can now. Look! I'm swallowing just fine."

Both Clayton and I had tears welling up as they continued. We were touched deeply that they made the effort to share with us what happened.

"The doctors insisted that she stay in the hospital for a few more days to run tests and try to figure out what happened. They had no answer but couldn't deny it was a miracle. Lois knew we were going on vacation to Canada and asked that we look you up and tell you that after you prayed, she was healed. She went home within a week and is living life as though she never had cancer."

When God performs a miracle, there are no loose ends. When He performs the supernatural, nothing is left undone.

And when His work is completed, we need to believe we receive and pray according to the Word. It's precisely the Word that gives us the authority to use the name of Jesus to stand against any giant.

And when facing those giants or encountering any difficulty, we might not know how to pray. That's when we remain still and wait, in faith, to hear from Him. He will reveal to us how to pray.

As He did with Clayton, we can be assured God will guide us.

And He shows us how and why in Romans 8:26: *"Likewise the Spirit also helps in our weaknesses. For we do not know what we should pray for as we ought, but the Spirit Himself makes intercession for us with groanings which cannot be uttered. Now He who searches the hearts knows what the mind of the Spirit is, because He makes intercession for the saints according to the will of God."*

And that intersession has no distance limitations. The next chapter illustrates this truth.

1. Do you believe you have the right and the authority to pray for a miracle? Why or why not?

2. Have you put your God-given authority into practice? What happened?

3. If God asked you to do something out of your comfort zone, would you hesitate to respond? If so, why?

4. Do you expect God to use you or do you think He only uses a chosen few? Why or why not?

Chapter 11
The Power of Praying in the Spirit

JIM'S PHYSICAL ATTACK was the last thing I expected. He was Clayton's childhood friend and they attended college together. And in recent years they became business partners.

In one of Clayton's frequent business travels, he was in South Africa on a buying trip for our diamond business. When Jim called that morning, I had no reason to suspect anything out of the ordinary.

"Hi, Carol. I guess Clay will be home tomorrow and back to the grindstone."

"I can't wait. Two weeks is a long time, especially for our son, Seth. Can you believe he is six months old already?"

"Why don't you stop over tonight? I went duck hunting on the weekend, and I'll give you a duck for Clay's homecoming dinner tomorrow."

"Perfect," I said, "you know how much he likes that."

Jim chuckled. "Just pop in anytime and I'll order a pizza for us."

I accepted the invitation. An adult conversation would be a welcome change after talking to a six-month-old for two weeks.

When I arrived at his house, Jim was his usual good-humored self. We chatted about how big Seth was getting and what a good baby he was.

"Would you mind if I feed him?" He asked.

Although Jim was a bachelor, he loved kids and hoped he would find the right gal someday to start a family.

After feeding him, Seth fell asleep, and Jim quietly laid him in his car seat.

"I'm getting hungry. Should we order pizza now?" I asked him.

We sat on the sofa together within a few feet of Seth's car seat so I could keep my eye on him in case he woke up.

"Carol," Jim said in a serious tone, "I think you know that I have always been attracted to you."

Attracted to me? Where did that come from?

"Clay is a nice guy and all," Jim blurted, "but he is a loser."

Was I hearing Jim right? Could he be joking? I assumed he was kidding. I gave him a puzzled look. "Jim, you're nuts."

"I'm serious. I could offer you much more than Clay ever could but if you don't want to leave him that doesn't mean we can't be more than friends."

Bam! There it was. He wanted to have an affair with no respect for the relationship he had with Clayton.

"I don't understand what you think is going on,'" I said, "but there is no way I am now or ever will be interested in you. I think I better leave."

As I stood up, Jim grabbed my arm and pulled me back onto the sofa.

"Let go of me you jerk." I tried to keep my voice low so Seth would stay asleep.

Jim's grip on my arm got tighter. He was well over six feet tall and frequently worked out in the gym.

My heart beat fast and my muscles tightened. I shook with a blend of fear and anger.

I screamed and blurted out, "Either you let me go or you're gonna be sorry." I had no clue what I meant by that; it seemed the appropriate thing to say.

I knew that was an empty threat, but no other defense came to me.

With an eerie grin, Jim pulled me towards him and said, "We'll see about that."

With one of his massive arms, he pushed me onto my back and held me down with his full weight.

Although anger in me grew, I felt helpless. The only defense would have to be supernatural. I was no match for this monster. In my spirit, I was asking God for help and knew He was my protector.

"Get off of me!" I screamed.

As Jim was positioning himself on top of me, I quickly drove my knee square into his groin. He let out a loud groan. I knew there would be no way I could have done that in the natural realm.

I needed to fight back for my safety and Seth's who woke up with an ear-splitting scream.

As Jim clutched himself in agony, with one swoop, I rolled out from under him, picked up my keys from the coffee table, and grabbed the car seat. I opened the front door and ran down the steps toward my car.

I didn't turn around. "Calm down. Calm down. Hold your hand steady so you can get the key in the ignition." I spoke out loud to help compose myself.

"Mommy is going to fix your seat in a moment." I tried to soothe Seth who had stopped crying but seemed agitated.

I placed the car seat in the front but didn't secure it. I didn't want to waste one second by checking to see if Jim was coming after me. I continued to talk out loud in the hope Seth would hear my soothing tone.

I drove a couple of blocks and pulled over. Then my fear turned to rage as I realized what I escaped. I took Seth out of his seat and held him close.

"I know you were scared to hear Mommy yell like that. But we're okay now. Daddy will be home tomorrow. He can't wait to see you. We love you so much. Everything's okay."

During the 30-minute drive home, I had the chance to figure out what to do. Should I tell Clayton? Should I keep quiet? Will I ever be able to be around Jim again?

The words Jim spoke were haunting me. "I've always been attracted, to you and I bet you feel the same way. Clay doesn't have to know. It'll be our secret." The thought made me shudder. I will not think about this again. I just can't.

A hot bath and a good night's sleep were what I needed to help put this entire evening behind me. I suspected it would take time before I could tolerate being in Jim's company but suppressing the incident would help.

There. Done. Over. It would remain a secret.

The next morning was bright, and I was thankful to have had a good night's sleep. Clayton would be tired from the 17-hour flight and anxious to get home.

Seth and I went to pick him up. From inside the terminal, I could see him approaching but his gait was hurried.

I thought that was odd. He is usually stiff on his feet after a long trip.

As he entered the terminal and I was within hearing distance he blurted, "Jim attacked you. Are you okay?"

"What?" I almost shouted. "Why would you say that?"

I clutched Seth not wanting him to feel any tension. As we got into the car I was in turmoil. Should I deny it? How did he know?

"I was flying from Johannesburg to London last night and sound asleep. I woke up suddenly with an intense burden to pray for you." Clayton's voice was unsteady and anxious.

It was becoming clear to me how he knew what happened. I couldn't deny it. He would know I was lying.

"I didn't have a clue how or what to pray for but the only means to release this pressure was to pray in the spirit until that burden lifted. After 45 minutes of praying this way, I felt the release."

Clayton continued as I stared straight ahead fighting back the tears and trying to stay composed.

"Then I asked God to show me what I was praying about," Clayton said, "In my spirit, God showed me what happened to you. Immediately fear overwhelmed me. But I knew I had authority over that fear, so I rebuked it in Jesus' name and it lifted. Then I fell back to sleep."

"Just like that?" I asked.

"Just like that."

I never doubted God's love for me. But at this precise moment, I sensed God wrapping me in His arms. Just like I had comforted and protected Seth, God sheltered His daughter.

I sat quiet, puzzled but at the same time relieved. My secret had been revealed. I had to share my side of the story.

As I recounted what happened the night before, Clayton's face grew tense and serious. His reaction concerned me; I am a peacemaker by nature. I didn't want this to destroy their friendship.

We figured out that at the very moment Jim was attacking me, Clayton was in prayer. He was somewhere between Johannesburg and London. I was in Minnesota.

Time zones don't matter. God's timing is always perfect.

"Please don't say anything to Jim," I begged Clayton, "I don't want to come between you guys, and you have to work with him."

Clayton reluctantly agreed but the friendship was never the same. When it came time to cut business ties, the relationship ended.

The night of the incident, I felt weak, helpless, and in danger. But Romans 8:26 says *"Likewise the Spirit also helps in our weaknesses. For we do not know what we should pray for as we ought, but the Spirit Himself makes intercession for us with groanings which cannot be uttered."* The literal Greek translation adds the words 'in articulate speech.' In other words, with understanding.

When we find ourselves in circumstances and don't know how to pray, we have the assurance that the Holy Spirit knows exactly what is happening and we allow Him to pray through us.

We may feel a heaviness regarding our children or loved ones. The Lord will bring someone to our mind who we know intimately or barely know. These are times when we need to exercise the gift of praying in the spirit to receive the answer. God gives us the assurance in our spirit that He interceded and answered our prayer. This reassurance comes when the burden lifts and often is replaced with joy.

According to 1 Corinthians 14:15, we have the right to ask God for the interpretation of what we have prayed in the spirit. It states: "What is the conclusion then? I will pray with the spirit, and I will also pray with the understanding."

People often attribute unusual strength to a rush of adrenaline but the Holy Spirit gives us what we need beyond our expectations. We can rest in that fact and stand on the Word that promises us protection. Peace comes back, faith grows, and fear disappears.

1. What does it mean to pray in the spirit?

2. Have you been in a situation when praying in the spirit seemed to be the only way to pray?

3. When you speak in tongues in prayer, do listen in your heart for the interpretation?

Chapter 12
The Prayer of Salvation

FIONA'S LONG BLONDE hair swayed from side to side with each step she took. She stopped at the spa's entrance "Here I am," she said, and I greeted her with a warm, welcoming hug.

Her smile was infectious. "Make me beautiful," she said. I explained the service packages offered. She wanted all of them, but the price was an obstacle.

"What can you offer me?" she asked.

"We could trade services."

I often suggested this to potential clients. It afforded me services ranging from house cleaning to dog sitting.

"Do you need an accountant?" she said. I had recently fired the last one and was getting desperate in my search for a trustworthy one.

She gave me a verbal resume. And her experience impressed me.

"Deal."

We hugged on that agreement.

Our friendship developed into a sisterhood. We had a bond of trust and confidentiality as she shared her battle with depression. It had been her secret. But now she had an avenue, safe enough to reveal her darkest thoughts.

As I listened to the details, I fought the urge to blurt out, "You need Jesus," but God cautioned me. Experience taught me His timing is perfect and pushing it might cause her to run.

At that time, I was close to the completion of my memoir, **Battered Hope**, and I needed a beta reader. That task would be an additional service Fiona could provide. She agreed. And her acceptance would benefit both of us. She would have the opportunity to subtly, yet clearly read the story of how God helped me through major traumas and gave me the strength to persevere.

In the meantime, since the tax season approached, we needed hours and hours of preparation for the year-end reports.

Fiona's help with this effort would be timely. After our lunch, I planned to spend the afternoon pouring over figures with her.

Once at the restaurant, I placed my menu on the table and waited for Fiona to order.

I glanced in her direction. As the menu in her hands shook, she gave a slight whimper.

I reached across the table and touched her hand. "Fiona, are you okay?"

She put the menu down and leaned toward me. "It's not fair. It's just not fair. It makes me so mad!"

Made her mad?

"I'm so sorry, Fiona," I said, "what did I do to upset you?"

She wiped the tears from her cheeks. "You didn't do anything. It's what they did to you."

I was still confused. "What are you talking about? Who did what to me?"

"All those people in your book. All those creeps who hurt you and tried to trash you. I've never met anyone who has had to endure so much pain."

Suddenly it was clear. She referred to the episodes in my memoir. I struggled with the answer. I shrugged my shoulders. "That was then, this is now," I said, "I'm over it."

She stared for a moment. "I don't get it. How could anyone treat another human being as they treated you?"

I smiled inwardly and wondered how she would handle the next eight chapters of the trauma she still had to read.

Would this be the right time to tell her about Jesus? No, not yet. God knew my heart's desire to see Fiona take the step and ask Him into her life. But I needed to be obedient to His timing.

I gave a quick chuckle. "You ain't seen nothin' yet, girlfriend. But, hey, look at me now." I pointed to myself grinning to help her see that I was a better person than the one she read about. She laughed.

"Let's order," I said, "I'm famished, and we have a lot of work ahead."

I was certain the time would come when I would share Jesus with her. But not today.

In the weeks that followed, she continued to read my manuscript. At times she commented about how strong I was, and I was glad she could understand that not only did I refrain from seeing myself as a victim, but more importantly, I could not have survived without God's help.

A couple of days later and tax deadlines drew closer, I called Fiona from the ferry line-up. "The ferry is on overload," I said, "and I am stuck waiting for at least three hours. Why don't you meet me here and we can go over everything in my car?"

She agreed. After an hour of delving into figures, I heard that still small voice I knew well. All He said was, "Now."

There was no doubt. It had to be now.

Fiona, do you remember a few weeks ago when you cried in the restaurant?" I asked. She lowered her head in embarrassment.

"No! Don't be silly," I assured her, "You shouldn't be ashamed. I was deeply moved by your compassion. I was only wondering if you remembered what you asked me that day."

She nodded. "Yup. I still wonder how you ever survived."

"The truth is, Fiona, I wondered that many times. It was only because God protected me, sustained me, and loved me through each circumstance," I said, "that's the reason I made it."

She raised her eyebrows encouraging me to continue. I did with no hesitation.

"I know how deeply you hurt, Fiona. I also know the medication only masks the pain you have been through. But God knows it too. He knows you intimately. Better than you know yourself. He wants nothing more than to have you recognize how much He loves you and for you to ask Him into your heart; into your life."

She sighed deeply. "I knew that's what you would say. I watched you. While I read your book, I knew you had an answer. And I figured someday you would share it with me."

I glanced up. There was the ferry, approaching the terminal and I chuckled inwardly at God's timing.

I looked into her eyes. "Fiona, would you like to ask Jesus into your life to give you the strength you need and to cleanse you from all your past, your guilt, your shame, your sin?"

"Yes," she nearly shouted. Her tears flowed as she asked Jesus to be her Lord and Savior and to forgive her sin.

"Now get out of the car," I said jokingly, "or else you will be going to the city with me."

After we gave each other a quick hug, I watched her sprint across the parking lot.

"Thank you, Lord. Thank you for Your perfect timing. Thank you for allowing me to lead my precious friend to You."

During the long trip on the ferry, I reflected on Fiona's life, her out-of-the-ordinary adventures, and her passion for what she did.

Recently she joined the local dragon boat club, and she loved being on the water. "Having the wind on my face," she had said, "and seeing so far into the horizon is like looking into the forever."

Her passion was rewarded when she qualified as a search-and-rescue volunteer with a perfect score. She delighted in moments at the helm, steering the boat while wearing silver rings– on all ten fingers.

But she was still committed to helping me with the tax reports. That afternoon in the ferry terminal, I had reminded her taxes were due on Monday. She promised to be at my office no later than noon the next day.

By one o'clock Sunday afternoon, she was an hour late already. I huffed. Where could she be?

I dialed her number several times. No answer. That irritated me more. Why wasn't she answering or calling me back?

It was 3:25 p.m. when my phone finally rang. Since I recognized her number, I answered curtly, "Finally! What took you so long?"

Silence.

"Hello?" I was hoping I had not offended her.

"This is Fiona's mother. Fiona was killed in a freak Coast Guard accident about three hours ago."

I burst out, "Are you sure?" I realized it was a stupid question. I dropped the phone on the floor. "NO! NO! NOOOOOOO!" I screamed.

Clayton ran into my office. I was on the floor crying, "Fiona is dead."

Details of what happened trickled in. Fiona and another female volunteer were killed. Fiona was the accountant of Community Services. The other woman managed our local radio station.

Early that Sunday morning, Fiona had received a phone call from the captain who wanted to do a practice run when the ocean rapids were at a peak. Fiona was certain she would be home in time to finish the taxes, so she agreed.

The captain's superior made it clear that he was not to take that risk. "It is extremely dangerous and unnecessary," he told the captain. But the captain argued that it would be the perfect time to train the new gals on how to manipulate the Zodiac in danger zones. Once again, his superiors forbade him to go. He didn't listen.

Normally when a Zodiac capsizes, it immediately flips back upright. But not this time. It became wedged between large rocks, trapping the two women volunteers under its rigid hull. Their seatbelts were caught, and their safety suits were tethered to the boat. When the boat flipped, they hit their heads hard on impact. Although the rest of the crew were able to escape, it was too late for Fiona and her friend.

The entire community attended the funeral. Through this tragedy, I was able to share with other Christian friends that they could rest assured Fiona knew Jesus. She was with Him forever and one day we would laugh together again.

Fiona's episode confirmed that God has our future in His hands. He orchestrated the meeting I had with Fiona at the ferry terminal. As the daughter of a pastor, I grew up going door-to-door in the neighborhood sharing Jesus. Many people enjoyed doing this. Not me. I was always uncomfortable. I felt as though I was forcing my beliefs onto someone who may not want to hear about them.

Yet, if I didn't share Christ, I felt guilty.

But then I learned a vital lesson. I learned how to follow the urging of the Holy Spirit when someone needed to hear about Jesus' love.

Opportunities Come in Unexpected Ways

As I drove on a busy interstate highway, I heard that familiar voice:

"Pass the car in your right lane and motion to the driver in the car next to you to pull over."

"What?"

I heard the instruction, but the idea was a bit puzzling. Ask someone who is traveling 70 miles an hour to pull over. The idea seemed impossible. Yet...the prompting persisted.

I pulled up beside the car in the right lane and motioned for the woman driver to pull onto the shoulder.

I stopped in front of her and got out. As I walked toward her car, I still had no idea what to say to her. I had no clue until I saw her tear-stained face.

I approached the driver's window and looked into her puffy eyes. "I stopped you today to tell you that God loves you. He suffered and died for you so that you could spend eternity with Him and live forever."

She stared for a moment; her brow wrinkled. "How could you possibly have known?"

"Known what?" I asked.

"I made my decision today to drive to the next bridge and jump off. I couldn't think of one reason why I should live another day. I hated myself."

The Holy Spirit's prompting was clear to me, this woman was ready to receive her salvation. On the shoulder of that highway, she asked Jesus into her heart. We exchanged phone numbers, and I assured her I would stay in touch.

Situations like this began to happen regularly. Each time I got into my car, I wondered who God had planned to send my way. Sometimes months passed but I was always ready.

And I waited with expectation because nothing is more exciting than to know the Master of the universe cares so much for every single person on this planet. I believe God orchestrates our lives for His purpose. As a result, sometimes our plans may change abruptly. That's because God's plans are better. When we begin to expect God to use us, we will see more opportunities than ever before.

Opportunities Come in Discomfort

One time that is forever embedded in my mind was further out of my comfort zone than normal.

One sunny morning, after I ordered breakfast on the ferry, I noticed a woman sitting in the cafeteria with her back to me.

She was scantily dressed, and tattoos covered the exposed parts of her body.

Right before I took my first bite of toast, God spoke to my heart. "Go talk to her."

"Talk to her? What would I say?"

I should have known better than to argue. I fought the urge to be judgmental. Yet, I still reasoned this young woman would have nothing in common with me, who seemed twice her age.

Reluctantly, I took slow steps toward her table. I had not yet seen her face. As I approached her from the back, I prepared to say, "I see we are headed in the same direction, maybe we could sit together."

But instead, I only got the first two words out when I saw her eyes. "I see....." and then I saw Jesus on her countenance. There is no way to explain it. There were a light and a joy in her eyes that seemed to shout out to me that she loved Jesus. I said, "I see you are a Christian."

Her eyes sparkled. "Yes, I am returning from a Bikers for Jesus rally in the mountains this weekend. That's where I asked Jesus into my heart."

I bent down and hugged her. "Tell me about yourself."

She related she had been an exotic dancer for years and her stage name was Heavenly. That was funnier than I had imagined. We laughed together. A few of her friends had decided to check out the rally and she tagged along.

I asked her if she had a Bible and she said she did not. Although the ferry trip was only 40 minutes long, I had time to get a Bible from my car to give her. I also asked her to promise to stay in touch.

As months went by, I watched her develop into a beautiful Christian woman who loved Jesus with all her heart.

I reflected on the sequence of events God had orchestrated, someone had planted the seed and I was able to help water it over the next few years.

Throughout this book, you have seen a wide range of circumstances that show you the benefits of being obedient when God says "Now." Not only do we bless others, but we reap incredible miracles.

1. **Do you think it is important to speak to everyone you know about Jesus? Why or why not?**

2. **The last time you led someone in the salvation prayer did you sense that person was ready to hear about Jesus before you prayed?**

3. **Have you ever hesitated to talk to someone about Jesus because you felt they were not ready to hear about Him? Or do you think it was fear that held you back?**

Chapter 13
Praying Out of Our Comfort Zone

CLAYTON SHOT TO his feet as across his desk, a large, brown rat stood on its hind legs. It hissed at him as if to say: "You're invading my territory."

Clayton yelled at the disgusting intruder, and it scurried into the back of the store.

Nothing we tried brought results. The rats continued to take over.

Our exclusive jewelry store had become infested with them. They chewed a hole into our ceiling from the restaurant next door. We were clueless as to what the attraction was in our store as we had no food products.

This continued for 13 months. Pest Control came once a week to collect the rats from the traps mounted in our ceiling tiles. They usually removed a minimum of 20 dead rodents. The stench of rotting flesh caused both of us to feel ill. On many days we had to close the store shortly after opening in the morning because the stench was overpowering on warm days.

Our business suffered. The gossip in the community was that we were closing. We tried all the recommended methods including ultrasonic sound waves, but nothing slowed them down — they continued to multiply.

Clayton contracted a severe rash on his arms from resting them on his desktop; the doctor confirmed it was from rodent residue.

We had no one to turn to. The landlady refused to repair the roof because of the expense. The restaurant next door also refused to correct the damages. Yet, when we approached the restaurant owner, he admitted there was a problem. "Don't tell anyone," she said, "but we bring our cat here every night."

Inspections by the health department were futile. The restaurant owners became aware of their visit in advance and hid the evidence.

Since we could no longer work under these conditions, we had no choice but to alert the landlady of our need to break our lease.

"I don't know what you are doing in that store to create such a problem, she said, "it's your responsibility to identify that and alleviate the problem."

Although she was wrong, legal fees to fight her weren't in the budget. We had searched for another location for a year and nothing would be vacant anytime soon. We considered closing our business but what would we do then?

We prayed. Nothing changed. We prayed some more.

The office for my business as a health coach was also located in our store. The day I walked into my office and saw maggots crawling on my desk, rage filled me. It was obvious I was going to have to stop one-on-one coaching.

Enough!

Since Clayton was out of town that day, I was in charge of the store. I locked the front door and drew the shades. With determination, I walked around the store and declared my authority and the

God-given rights I possessed over anything that was trying to destroy our business and our health.

I spoke out loud. "Father, I know that Your Word declares in 1 John 4 that greater is He who is in me than he who is in the world. I stand against any demonic assignment on us or our business. I take authority against the enemy and command these rodents to leave our premises and never return."

Bam!

Instantly in my spirit, I felt a sharp twinge. It felt like a rebuke. I almost lost my footing from the shock of it. And then, in a gentle and soft voice, I heard God speak to my spirit.

"Why haven't you thanked Me for the rats?"

"What?" Was I hearing correctly?

"But, Lord, I have prayed the scripture thanking You that all things work together for my good."

Again, I heard that inner voice say, "Why haven't you thanked Me for the rats?"

I didn't know how I was going to form those words out of my mouth to thank God for rats but as I humbly hung my head, I remembered Philippians 4:6 *"Be anxious for nothing, but in everything by prayer and supplication, with thanksgiving let your requests be made known unto God. And the peace of God, which surpasses all understanding, will guard your hearts and minds through Christ Jesus."*

I had complained. I cried. I even begged. But I had not thanked God for orchestrating every part of my life — even the rats. His ways are much higher than my imagination.

"Lord, please forgive me. I know that You orchestrate my life. I know my life is in Your hands. I know that You are fully aware of what is happening. I have been lax in thanking You for that. I don't understand why the rats are here, but You do."

"Thank you, Heavenly Father, for confirming that I need to trust You completely and be patient."

As I began to praise Him for Who He is and thank Him for His love and protection, the anxiety lifted. I became excited and realized God was in control — not me. He would fulfill His promises. God did not want us to fail. My job was to trust Him.

If the rats played a part in that scenario, I needed to trust God that He knew what He was doing. He is the giver of good gifts to His children.

In 3 John 1:2, it says, "I wish above all things that you may prosper and be in health, even as your soul prospers."

The next day, the owner of the strip mall across the street walked into our store. He asked if we were interested in renting an additional parking space as he also owned the town's parking lot.

We jokingly responded, "No, but we would like to rent another spot if there would ever be one available."

"I'll have one soon." He said.

Could that be true, I wondered.

"One of my tenants would like to divide their large space in half," he said, I am renovating it and it will be available in about a month. I was planning to put an ad in the paper this week, but if you want it, it's yours."

My thoughts raced to yesterday's events when the Lord pointed out my doubts. Could God be answering my prayer of praise by bringing this offer so quickly? I was sure of it.

The square footage would be similar to our current space. The renovation would make it nearly brand new, and its location was on the preferred sunny side of the street.

The monthly cost was equal to half of our current payment for the rat-infested, run-down building, on the dark side of the street where the public rarely walked.

In preparing for the move, miracles happened each step of the way.

A moving company quoted us $1,000 to move our 3,500-pound safe for a distance of a few hundred feet.

God knew our financial struggle, so He sent the local car towing company. They moved it for $60. It was great entertainment for on-lookers to watch a huge safe being driven down the main street swinging from the winch on the back of a tow truck.

The layout of the new store was unique and conducive to displaying the various types of art we also carried. Every aspect of the new store exceeded our wildest expectations. We were in our previous location for 11 years and are well-known in the community. Yet every day in the new store we had at least ten new customers who had only recently discovered us. Our business soared.

It is certainly easier to be thankful when we are on the other side of a traumatic situation. But when we are thankful during the trial of faith, we reap the full blessing of what God intended for us. When we choose to trust Him and praise Him as He asks us to do, it becomes a testimony of His faithfulness.

Whenever I face a situation that seems insurmountable, I remember how God taught me to thank Him for the rats.

1. **Have you stepped out of your comfort zone when you prayed? If so, how?**

2. **Do you make an effort to make your requests known to God through the prayer of thanksgiving? If not, how can you improve on that?**

Chapter 14
Beyond Our Shame

FOR YEARS, I had been ashamed of many phases of my life. My husband, Clayton, and I made numerous embarrassing mistakes throughout our journey. They were too painful to admit to our Christian friends who respected us.

As a result, I was determined to keep silent about our past. I tried to hide all those rugged circumstances. I became masterful at the art of avoiding personal questions. I managed this by controlling the conversation to remain one-sided. I would ask questions and encourage others to share their stories. This would protect me from revealing my own.

But this mindset changed with an unexpected incident.

Some years back, our daughter, Rochelle, asked us to babysit her new puppy, a miniature Dachshund named Louis Vuitton.

"I'll be gone for two weeks," she said, "but Louie won't be any problem for you. He loves staying with his gramma and papa."

How do you say no to that? Of course, we committed to caring for him. But, instead, that little dog took care of preparing a gigantic revelation for me.

One cool evening, Clayton and I settled on the living room sofa. Suddenly, an awful commotion came from the upstairs bedroom.

Tha-Thump. Tha-Thump. Something heavy dragged down the stairs.

Using his teeth, tiny six-month-old Louie pulled his large, hard-sided Louis Vuitton carrier down the fourteen stairs, one step at a time.

With a defiant glance, Louie looked toward us on the sofa. After placing his case in the center of the living room, he wagged his tail and scurried back up the stairs.

Clayton turned to me. "What in the world do you think he is doing?"

"I have no idea," I said, "but I think we are about to be entertained."

In anticipation, I was ready to make popcorn and take in this new doggie show. We watched in amazement as Louie made numerous trips dragging his possessions down the stairs. First his blankie, then his bowl, his bone, his ball, and his sweater. On his final trip, he brought his leash.

This show was not over. Standing on his hind legs, he could barely reach the top of the carrier. But he jumped and jumped, never giving up until each of his items dropped inside the bag.

Now what?

Clayton and I cheered at Louie's endless attempts to jump into the bag.

"C'mon, Louie, you can do it," we chanted. He panted from exhaustion, but he refused to give up.

One final leap and he landed head-first into his packed 'suitcase.'

I shook my head wondering what would happen next. "Look! He's not done yet."

Clayton laughed when he realized the reason for Louie's efforts. "He's trying to zip it closed from the inside."

"I just figured it out," I said, "he's packing his suitcase just like his mommy did when she left for her trip. He's planning to go find her."

Early the next morning, we unzipped the carrier and placed Louie on the floor. He ran around the house as fast as he could but soon realized Mommy was not there. He was still at Gramma's house and Rochelle was nowhere.

He looked at us as if to say, "Gramma, why isn't mommy here?"

For the next fourteen days, Louie entertained us with unusual and funny antics. I kept a daily journal written from his perspective. Once finished, I had it printed with pictures of each day's story and gave it to Rochelle for Christmas.

She laughed as she turned each page. Then she paused and gave me a serious look. "Mom, when are you going to write your own story?"

I dropped into the nearest chair with that revelation. The message was clear. Louie showed such tenacity and determination to do nearly the impossible. The lesson was for me. I needed to apply that same courage.

For over ten years Rochelle had been asking me to write my story as a reminder of God's love for her generation. She knew many young women who would relate to the trauma I had been through. She wanted them to realize that no matter how difficult life can be, with God's help, they can overcome.

I repented before the Lord and confessed to Rochelle too. That night, I prayed, "Forgive me for my blindness. I only saw how it would affect me. I missed the fact my mistakes could minister to others and help them conquer their own."

Like Louie, I gathered courage and resolve. During the ten years it took to write my memoir, I had to dredge up ugliness and pain that was deeply buried. But momentum built as I pondered on the purpose of relating my story.

Soon, the excitement was built at the thought of offering hope to those who had been battered and beaten by life.

I completed the book and finally, the day arrived. I opened the box of my first batch of *Battered Hope,* in print. I pulled a copy out and clutched it to my chest. "Thank You, Lord."

But it didn't take long before the intruder called **doubt** tried to barge in.

I glanced at Clayton. "What if no one buys it?"

"You're not trusting God." He said with no hesitation, "He is going to use your story to bring others to Christ. But always remember the bottom line of anything we do is this: If only one person is encouraged or only one person accepts Jesus as a result, we have done our part."

His wise words would keep me focused as I worked through the hurdles in the marketing and selling process.

Only six weeks later I received a pleasant surprise. A message came to me through Facebook from a woman named Oxana.

"I am contacting you because I recently purchased your book through Amazon."

Although the message came after midnight, I immediately responded.

"Thank you. I hope you enjoy it. Where do you live?"

"I live in Ukraine, but I am originally from Russia. I am enjoying your story but not the message. You say you believe in God, but I know there is no God."

"What makes you say that Oxana?"

"I was raised in Russian royalty," she wrote, "and forced to marry someone I didn't know. He beat me which caused me to miscarry my baby. After the birth of my next baby, he continued to abuse my young son and me."

"I'm so sorry to hear that but God knows everything you went through. He loves you and wants to heal your pain."

I imagined her laughing out loud as she scoffed at my trust in a God whom she insisted didn't exist.

Oxana told how she escaped Russia when her son was young. She went into hiding losing her royalty status as well as any inheritance she deserved. She related that her strength came from within herself and had nothing to do with God.

We continued our written conversations online. I asked her questions about her life, and she shared the horrific experiences she had endured.

With each story, she strongly emphasized that if there was a God, He would never allow such pain.

Fifteen nights in a row we chatted online. She would read a chapter of my book and then discuss it with me that evening. She began to soften as she realized so many of her experiences paralleled my own.

Her questions included, "Why didn't you get angry or seek revenge? How could you forgive people who hurt you severely? Why didn't you blame your God when you lost your son?"

God gave me the wisdom to choose my words carefully. The message was the same every night. "God knows your name. God loves you. He cares about you. He died for you. When you ask Jesus into your life, He will not only give you joy but the promise of living forever with Him."

I gave her the verse in Jeremiah 29:11 which says: *"For God knows the thoughts that He thinks towards you, thoughts of peace and not of evil, to give you a future and a hope."*

Her initial comment: "That is the most senseless, unintelligent reasoning I have ever heard."

But as time went on, she asked, "How do you know God exists? How do you know He cares about you?"

I always responded the same way. "It's a matter of believing God loves you. He created you and wants to spend eternity with you."

Suddenly, with no warning, the messages stopped. I tried contacting her through the same channel but there was no response. I had to trust God that the seeds I planted would stay with her.

Two weeks later, I received this email:

"You don't know me, but I believe you knew my mother, Oxana."

I quickly read through the letter and then read it repeatedly.

"I don't know if this means anything to you, but my mother died two weeks ago. She died in her sleep, and she had two things in her hands. In one hand she held your book close to her chest. This is where I got your email address. In her other hand was a short note which I don't understand but I hope you will. It said, 'I love Jesus.' I read the many conversations you had with her on Facebook. I strongly felt that I should contact you and let you know what happened."

Oxana is one among many who asked Jesus into their heart after reading **Battered Hope**. Someday we will meet people we never met on earth but who came to know Jesus through our words.

Each one of us has a story to tell. I encourage you to find a way to share your story, your miracle. All the fears of embarrassment and shame of our past are quickly forgotten when we realize God can use our past to brighten someone else's future.

God expects us to do so. In my case, He used a miniature Dachshund to get my attention.

This is a book about miracles. The greatest miracle we will ever see in our lifetime is the miracle of salvation.

1. **When you are positive that God asked you to do something, is it difficult to wait for confirmed results?**

2. **Have you had miracles in your life? Do you share them with others?**

Chapter 15

It's Never Too Late

A COUPLE OF years ago, I received an email from Rob, a television executive producer who wanted to share his story on my show. Before I finished reading his email my spirit quickened. The message from the Lord was clear. "You need to go pray for him."

Pray for him? Why? Rob was simply presenting a query to be a guest on my show, "Never Ever Give Up Hope." Since I interview ordinary people who have survived extraordinary hardships, I assumed Rob would have such a story.

I knew nothing about him or where he lived. I also didn't understand why this prompting from God was so strong. But I couldn't dismiss that still small voice urging me to meet with him.

When I realized he lived in a city where I would soon be speaking, things began to make sense. I emailed Rob telling him I was a Christian. I also shared that I didn't know why, but I sensed God wanted me to visit him. I would be in his city soon for a speaking engagement.

"I understand if you find this to be uncomfortable," I said to him, "and if you rather not meet, I understand that too."

Two days passed. No response. I wondered if Rob changed his mind about being on my show. Or perhaps wanted nothing to do with a woman who invited herself to his home.

Then his email arrived. I wept as I read it.

"Just when I was beginning to wonder if God cared, I received your email." He wrote. "There is no way you could have known that our four-year-old daughter has been diagnosed with stage four pediatric cancer. This is a rapidly growing cancer and children rarely survive more than a few months. The doctors give us little hope."

My heart beat fast with amazement at God's timing. I fought the urge to go see them immediately. "I'll be speaking in your area and could see you on my way home on December 13 at two in the afternoon."

He agreed.

Early in the morning of the day I was to visit Rob, I realized I did not have his address or phone number. This wouldn't be a problem, I reasoned, as I would email him and get that information.

I powered up my laptop, but nothing happened. I tried everything but it crashed. Panic set in for a moment. This glitch would cause a delay in my travel to the venue which was several miles away. I simply could not be late.

Finally, I gained access to a computer in the hotel. Success! I got Rob's phone number and googled his address. My meeting ran overtime so I called to tell him I would be an hour late. The call went straight to voicemail, but I wasn't concerned because he expected my visit.

My mind was still relishing in the results of the event where I had spoken. Not only was God's love for those women palpable, but I was elated to see what God would do for Rob and his little girl.

My GPS directed me to his neighborhood, but as I drew close there was no street by that name. I called Rob. Again, it went straight to voicemail.

Even more than before, I was certain God was about to perform a miracle. Anticipation grew. If there had been any doubt, it was now erased

I drove up and down the same streets thinking that my GPS made a mistake. But each time it directed me back to the same place. It was time to begin praising — praise would break through this dilemma and bring clarity to what I was to do next.

It was now after four in the afternoon. Although the sky had turned dark, I lifted the Lord in praise for who He is and thanked Him for bringing me to this place. I thanked Him for His Word and declared He alone could heal this little girl.

Joy filled me and I swallowed hard when I heard the Lord speak.

"Get out of the car, walk around the street sign, and look at it from a different direction." That instruction seemed odd, but I obeyed. Even in the dark, I was able to see a street sign laying in the ditch. Although it had been embedded in cement, there it was, on its side.

I assumed someone had hit it with their car. It didn't matter. God directed me and I was standing on the corner of Rob's house.

It was now over two hours later than when we were to meet. I knocked on the door. A young man answered. "Hi, may I help you?"

"Hi. I'm Carol?"

I questioned if I was at the right house because he seemed shocked that I was there.

"Didn't you get my message?" Rob asked.

I glanced at my phone. "No, I don't have any messages from you. Didn't you get my messages?"

Rob checked his phone and confirmed he didn't see any calls or messages from me.

"You tried to call me?" I asked.

He nodded slowly. "My daughter took a turn for the worse this morning and she is in the hospital."

Tears formed in his eyes. "I had to come home to pick my son up from school. I called you to say that you shouldn't bother because it was too late, anyway."

"Rob, God never makes a mistake. He knew what time I was going to arrive at your home. He knew that your daughter would not be here. He knew I would be late and that I would have difficulty finding your house. He knew that somehow our phone messages went into cyberspace. Yet here I am obeying what God originally told me to do. May I come in?"

He looked a little startled, but he stepped aside, allowing me to enter. After engaging in small talk, I asked him for the specifics. As he shared his demise, I felt fear grip his heart.

He shared how he was a man of strong faith, but the battle was more than he could understand or handle. Both he and his wife were spent. The prognosis had taken its toll.

As he talked, once again I got excited. God's timing is always perfect. He is never late. I relayed that to Rob and told him he had nothing to fear. God didn't send me there to pray amiss. He had a plan and I was a messenger sent to bring Rob and his family a message of hope and healing.

We spent over ninety minutes talking as I shared several stories of healing with him. I sensed that he was catching a glimpse of what God was about to do.

I held his hands in mine. Tears fell as I praised God for who He is and for what He was about to do. I thanked Him for sending me there to encourage and pray with Rob. I asked God to confirm that to Rob's heart. And I thanked God for healing his child.

When I opened my eyes, Rob was smiling through his tears and he said, "This has never happened to me before but as you were praying, I believe I had a vision."

"What did you see?" I asked him.

"I saw my daughter in a beautiful dress. She looked about 17 years old, and I think she was in her graduation dress."

I let out a joyous laugh as he continued, "I have a friend who paints portraits. I am going to have him paint this picture as I describe it to him. I will hang it on my daughter's wall to remind us daily that God is our healer and I know I will one day see her in her graduation dress. For the first time since the diagnosis, all fear has gone. I know in my gut that she is healed."

When Rob called me a few days later, we cried together. The test results revealed that she was completely cancer-free. But the doctors wanted to be sure the cancer would never return. This child had to endure extensive prevention treatments which were extremely painful throughout the next 18 months. If the parents refused the treatments, the state could press charges and they would lose their parental rights.

Today, she remains cancer-free and is an encouragement to many families who are terrified as they struggle with a similar scenario.

As you read these stories, please realize that obeying God when He asks you to do something may often be out of your comfort zone. You may question why God is asking you when you don't feel equipped. Or you may ask how you possibly could go about it.

Boldness comes with the first step. And it's needed for each step of the way. I could have said "Forget it!" when I could not find Rob's house, or when I couldn't find his phone number. But the experience taught me never to stop when God gives me a task.

All we need to do is trust Him and He will supply everything we need.

When I was in my twenties God spoke to my heart, "Are you someone the Holy Spirit can trust?" Taken aback and not understanding the question at the time, I said "Yes." Clarity came later when I acted on that promise.

Have you ever felt God was asking you to step out of your comfort zone?

Have you ever been in a similar situation and had to decide to follow through...or forget it?

If you quit, why? Was it fear? Did you ever think 'What do I have to lose?'

1. **If you are sure of something God asked you to do, how do you overcome the fear?**

2. **How do you conquer the doubts?**

Chapter 16
Believe That You Receive

IT WAS A cool Sunshine Coast day on November 27, 2012. Clayton sat at his desk while I stood at the front counter of our jewelry store. Suddenly, our 31-year-old son, Jason, popped his head into the front door. He glared at us. "Just so you know," he said with stern conviction in his voice, "I hate you and never want to see you again."

Initially, I assumed it was a joke as he often teased us. I laughed out loud and said, "Okay, see you tomorrow."

And he was gone. Not for the day. But for the next eight-plus years.

Nothing made any sense. Why did Jason say that?

Clayton and I waited two days, but we did not hear from him. This was unusual because he was also our employee. We drove to his house, walked to the front door, and through the side window, we saw our grandbabies playing in the living room. My heart smiled at the scene.

Jason answered. He stepped out and closed the door behind him. His face was stiff with a strange grin. "Odd you should stop by," he said with words as sharp as his glare, "as I was sitting here deciding how I was going to kill you."

My knees weakened. I became dizzy, life seemed to be sucked out of me. All I could do was grip my husband's arm for support.

"I don't believe there is a God," Jason said with a matter-of-fact tone, "Now, I would appreciate it if you would just leave."

The door slammed shut. Our feet were frozen in place. I struggled to believe what we just heard and bit my lip to keep my tears from flowing.

Only a few days prior we had celebrated our 40th wedding anniversary. Our daughter arranged a gala anniversary affair more elaborate than our wedding. We rejoiced in all our blessings. Our son thanked us for being great parents and grandparents to his young boys. He told us how much he loved us and thanked us for graciously accepting his wife as our daughter.

On the way home from the party, my heart still rejoiced as I turned to Clayton and said, "I don't think I have ever been or could ever be any happier than I am right now."

Little did I know that only three days later, my world would be shattered. I could not process my emotions. Too many questions and no answers. Guilt overcame any sound reasoning. What had I done? Where did we go wrong? Why was Jason doing this?

Jason's behavior also impacted his sister, Rochelle. A few days later, she called and cried on the phone for 45 minutes, her words drowned in her sobs.

"She may need to be hospitalized," Rochelle's husband informed us, "Jason said some undeserved and hateful things to her."

None of us could figure out what motivated Jason to cut himself off from us.

As we spent Christmas with Rochelle and her family, there was an obvious void. All the unopened gifts for Jason and his family were under the tree. A few superficial chuckles interrupted the tears.

No closure.

But we're not alone in this journey. For those who lose a child through death, the pain is like no other. Yet, losing Jason this way was different. There was no reason. There was no closure.

We knew we were good parents. Yet, our friends began to view us as though we had done some terrible wrongs to make our son despise us. Or perhaps we had given him reasons to toss us aside emotionally. Their assumptions may have included some imagined shortcomings on our part.

When one loses a child through estrangement, there are no flowers or comfort given. There is no church service to help bring closure. People do not rally around you and bring you meals to help you get through those days or send cards of encouragement to help you through those moments when getting out of bed to face reality is more than you can bear.

Instead of celebrating Mother's Day, birthdays, and Father's Day, they become painful reminders of their child's absence. Rejected parents have few places to turn. They often feel isolated and embarrassed. They carry shame with a sense of helplessness to rectify the situation.

They are very aware of people who talk about them behind their backs - blaming their parents. You hear the whispers. "No good parent would ever have their child turn against them — surely they had done something to cause the separation."

What If?

There are many hurdles, and some are rarely overcome. When an adult child abandons their parents or as in my case, the entire family, the "what ifs" and "how-coulds" never stop.

Parents hope to move forward. But taking that step could mean giving up hope of his/her return. So, the option is to hang on. Thus, the risk of that growth is often stifled.

As one dear friend told me, "This journey is like living the grieving process but never seeing it end."

The day Jason stepped out of his front door was the last time we saw him face-to-face. As of this writing, he lives in the same town as we do. Our store is located on the main street downtown, so we see him walk past occasionally. He avoids looking in the window. If he spots one of us, his pace quickens. That reaction on his part turns the knife, reopening the wound in my heart again.

I experienced what it feels like to have your heart broken. The pain was intense. Losing a child is a journey of grief no one wants to travel. Your heart never totally heals, and you live for the memories hoping they will never fade.

Like many families, we suffered great losses in our lives. This was different. Many emotions paint the episode -- rejection, fear, pain, heartbreak, remorse, loneliness, guilt, and others.

According to the Mayo Clinic and the American Heart Association, many factors contribute to a condition known as Broken Heart Syndrome. They believe the condition is brought on by an adrenaline rush that happens shortly after a severely stressful situation. The left ventricle of the heart takes on a cone-like shape that resembles the shape of a pot the Japanese use to capture an octopus called "tako-tsubo" which means "fishing pot for trapping an octopus."

"Tako-tsubo Cardiomyopathy" is now Broken Heart Syndrome's medical name.

Wikipedia defines it as a sudden temporary weakening of the myocardium (the muscle of the heart). This weakening can be triggered by emotional stress such as the loss of a loved one. Stress cardiomyopathy is a well-recognized cause of acute heart failure.

Two of the most common causes of Broken Heart Syndrome are the loss of a spouse or a child. Scientists have shown that after such an incident, heart attack risks increased to 21 times higher than normal within the first day and were almost six times higher than normal within the first week. Anything short of bringing the loved one back does little to console them.

Questions are never answered. Had we loved our son too much? Not enough? I knew he wasn't happy in some areas of his life, but we supported him in whatever he did. My grandchildren were ripped from my heart at six months and two and a half years old. I did not have the chance to watch them grow up, bake cookies for them, read and play with them or hug them.

In the years that followed, it seemed my grief deepened, and my husband's anger did as well. He looked at our son as ungrateful for everything we did for him. We set him up in business. We hired his wife to work in our store. We gave and gave and then gave some more. We probably gave too much. But he was our adopted son who we knew had rejection issues, so we poured extra love and attention into him.

The Cycle of Grief

In my experience, there are no 'stages of grief.' There are cycles of grief. Just when you think you've moved from shock to anger to acceptance or any of the stages in between, another anniversary or a shared experience, or even a special sound or smell triggers a memory and the whole process starts all over again.

My suggestion to parents who have lost a child is to be patient with themselves. Grief is a strange companion.

I knew that firsthand. Grief was my companion. No matter how happy I was or what I managed to accomplish, I sensed the abyss - the emptiness, the loneliness, the......hole.

A few of Jason's friends told us they did not understand it. They had envied the relationship Jason had with us. In their youth, we were the 'go-to' house — the house where kids hung out and felt safe.

They tried to reason with Jason, but he turned away from them. He had bought the lie in his mind and hardened his heart against us.

Fetal Alcohol Syndrome (FAS)

Our doctor told us, "It is not unusual for a child with FAS to abandon his adoptive family in young adulthood. These children feel rejected and want their new parents to feel that rejection."

He continued, "There is rarely any warning and often the adoptee does not understand why he wants to leave. But his relationship with you is a constant reminder that his mother did not want him."

Hearing those words brought little comfort. But they did bring some understanding. It also helped me to grasp why Jason was jealous of his sister — our biological child.

The Turning Point

At some point during the first two years, I realized how my companion of grief was a liar. I, too, was believing a lie. I had to change my method of thinking. I was teaching one thing and living another.

"Train up a child in the way he should go and when he is old he will not depart from it." Proverbs 22:6 It is a declaration. It is not a suggestion.

Joshua 24:15 says *"As for me and my house, we will serve the Lord."* Again, a firm declaration of God's promises.

I began to pray the answer. The more I prayed the Word, the stronger my faith grew. I knew God had a plan for my life and my son's life. This was no surprise to Him. My duty was to believe what God had promised. I needed to make all my petitions in light of thanksgiving.

I became excited as I envisioned my son worshiping God. I was seeing him as God saw him. My doubts lifted. My fears were erased. The pain began to heal.

My mother's heart cried with tears of joy. I asked God to forgive my doubts. It was merely a matter of time and that was in God's hands alone.

Another Step

Two years ago, I walked into our local post office. To my surprise, there was Jason with his two little ones. We heard that he left his first wife and remarried a widow with five children. They had two more children and I surmised these two were two more of my precious grandchildren.

Jason glanced at me and turned away.

I still turned toward him. "Hi, Jason. These two must be your little girls."

Jason stared forward. "One is a boy," he said in a gruff voice.

I looked closer at the baby he had in his arms. "Oh, yes, I see that now. Sorry about that." I smiled at both little ones. "You are both so cute."

After completing my transaction at the counter, I headed toward my car. Through the rear-view mirror, I watched Jason lift the children into their car seats. He had always been such a gentle soul who loved children. As I watched, I thanked God he was such a good daddy.

Moments later he drove away, and I burst into tears. The emotion of those past few moments summoned tender memories. My hands shook with excitement and joy. I had seen my grandbabies. They were in good hands.

I believed God would use this moment in Jason's life as a trigger for good. I realized I too had grown. As dark thoughts tried to bring up old pain, I chose to ignore them. Instead, I thanked God that His timing, not mine, was perfect.

Hope is Alive

Years swept by. On Sunday, July 26, 2020, my friend called. "Jason was in church today."

"What?" I shouted into the phone.

"He was there with four of his children. He asked to speak to me after the service. He wanted to register his kids for daycare."

My heart raced. I had many questions. Her conversation with Jason was short, but he told her that he now had temporary custody of his two children from his first marriage. My mother's heart knew that this was a positive step for all involved and I tried to control myself. Surely, he would be contacting us soon.

As quickly as that thought came, the desire to attend that church the following Sunday grew. Yet, I realized that God's timing, not my timing, was not to be manipulated. This was a huge step in the right direction, and I did not want to mess it up.

For the next two Sundays, Jason attended church with his four children. Then Covid-19 prevented church gatherings. A few months passed and I continued to thank God for speaking to my son — for bringing him to this place. Only good could come of this and I needed to be patient.

Restrictions were lifted and Jason returned to the Sunday services for two weeks before they were once again shut down. The last time he attended, my friend was leading the praise and worship service and saw Jason drop to his knees, weeping before God, with his hands raised.

Joy Visits

Uncontainable joy. There are no descriptive words to explain what was happening in my heart. My prayers were answered.

Waiting is rarely easy. I had to choose to protect myself from negative or anxious thinking. The Bible has a Helmet Law. The suit of armor in Ephesians Six tells us to put on the armor. It is our means of defense against the enemy. Our three defensive weapons which we discussed in previous chapters are the Name, the Word, and the Blood.

Our defensive armor is the Belt of the Gospel of Truth, the Breastplate of Righteousness, the Shield of Faith, the Shoes of the Preparation of Peace, and the Helmet of Hope. Hope protects the mind. A helmet will do you no good unless you put it on.

Our Protection

When we speak scriptures over our lives, we are protecting our minds from negativity. The Helmet of Hope protects our mind — how? With God's Word and positive responses to the negativities we hear.

Faith resides in your spirit and hope resides in your mind. That's why in the battlefield of our minds our thoughts war against hope.

As we see statistics, watch the news, observe our finances diminishing, and face our loved one's illnesses, these all attack in a real way. And, if we allow them, circumstances can crush our hope.

The Key

Thoughts come from three primary sources:

1. Our senses — sight, hearing, touch, taste, and smell. We see the news, we hear something negative, etc.

2. Our subconscious memories remind us of what happened the last time.

3. The spiritual world — both from God and the devil. Learning to control our thoughts through scripture is the KEY to holding onto hope for our future good.

Jeremiah 29:11 says, *"For I know the thoughts that I think toward you, says the Lord, thoughts of peace and not of evil (harm), to give you a future and a hope."*

Know that God's Word is true. Do not be swayed by circumstances. Pray the answer for your family. He will restore what was taken away. This is the prayer in scripture I pray over my children and grandchildren:

I bow my knees to the Father of our Lord Jesus Christ from whom the whole family in heaven and earth is named, that He would grant you, according to the riches of His glory, to be strengthened with might through His Spirit in the inner man, that Christ may dwell in your hearts through faith; that you, being rooted and grounded in love, may be able to comprehend with all the saints what is the width and length and depth and height to know the love of Christ which passes knowledge; that you may be filled with all the fullness of God.

"Now to Him who is able to do exceedingly abundantly above all that we ask or think, according to the power that works in us, to Him be glory in the church by Christ Jesus to all generations, forever and ever. Amen." Ephesians 3:14 – 21.

The next time disturbing facts attack you, let God's Word settle the truth about your situation. And as the Holy Spirit bears witness to the truths you believe, the facts will change and you will receive your miracle.

When you ask yourself, "Do I have enough faith for this situation?" you have already put faith as a hindrance between you and Jesus' finished work. The more you focus on your faith, the more faith seems to slip away. But if you focus on the finished work of Christ and see God's grace toward you, God sees that as faith.

Never allow the unbelief of anyone to nullify the effect of your prayer of faith. Please recall the story of Peter in chapter two of this book. I walked into his hospital room with twelve people. I wondered if anyone in that room believed there would be a miracle that day. Some of them seem perturbed that I was giving false hope to Peter's wife. His mother appeared angry I was there.

But I was not concerned about what anyone was feeling or believing. I knew God sent me there. I knew God gave me the gift of faith needed for that moment. I knew there would be a miracle.

"For assuredly, I say to you, whoever says to this mountain, 'Be removed and be cast into the sea,' and does not doubt in his heart, but believes that those things he says will be done, he will have whatever he says.

Therefore, I say to you, whatever things you ask, when you pray, believe that you receive them, and you will have them." Mark 11:23 – 24

Believe Before You See the Manifestation

You must believe you already have it before you see it.

It is imperative to know there are two kinds of truth: sense-knowledge truth and revelation truth.

Sense knowledge is self-explanatory. It is what we see or feel. When we are in pain or sick, our senses tell us. There is no doubt. We can see it. We feel it. It is the absolute truth.

However, we cannot physically see the things of the spirit. But that realm is very real. What we sense in that realm is revelation truth. This is the realm where God operates in our lives. This is the realm He speaks to us. Everything we need has been provided for us in the spirit realm.

The Bible says: *"God is a Spirit. They that worship Him must worship Him in spirit and in truth"* John 4:24. Whose truth? Our sense-knowledge truth is telling us we are hurting. But God's truth found in His Word tells us He has made provision for us.

It's already been done for us. He has blessed us. When we can grasp that reality and tap into what our spirit is telling us rather than what our carnal mind is saying, then it is easy for us to believe it.

Whether we see the answer or not, does not mean that it is not there. When sense-knowledge truth contradicts revelation-truth or the Word, then we must choose to walk by revelation-truth. Choose to walk by what God says not by what our natural senses tell us.

What is in the spiritual realm is made real in the natural realm through faith. Repeat that out loud: What is in the spiritual realm is made real in the natural realm through our faith. Faith will grasp that truth and create the reality of it in our life. This is beyond our natural thinking which is precisely why God says to walk by faith and NOT by sight.

If you are sick in bed and you ask your physical body if it is healed, how would it respond? You are basing that report on how your body feels, what the thermometer says, or what the doctor told you. If you asked people around you if you were healed, what would they say? They would tell you that the fever has gone to your 'head' and you need to sleep it off and get better soon.

But the Word says in Romans 3:4 that God is truth and every man a liar. Choose to believe what God's Word is telling you. Choose to believe spirit-revelation truth. Choose to believe God rather than what you are feeling.

Give Thanks

When we believe that God has promised what we need, He will supply; we will not be anxious. We will pray a prayer of thanksgiving; thereby letting our petitions be made known to Him by thanking Him for the answer He has already provided.

When I was about seven years old, I had a large growth on my neck. It was ugly and scary. The doctor said that it would have to be removed surgically because it could be cancer. He could not make any promises that surgery would completely remove it.

My dad relayed his faith to me and told me that God was my healer, and He would remove that growth. In my youth, I did not understand why I was prepped for surgery. But my dad did. As the surgeon was about to cut into that lump, right before his eyes, it disappeared. Daddy told me that I was healed from the moment he prayed for me. And he added that was when he started to thank God for my healing.

The doctor was the man who needed to witness that miracle. My dad knew it was already done.

This is how I can thank God and praise Him that my son, my prodigal, will come home. God will restore the relationship. God will heal the pain. God's ways are far above my thoughts. What He has promised He will fulfill. My job is to trust the truth of God's Word and I will see it manifested.

"That the trial of your faith, being much more precious than of gold that perisheth, though it be tried with fire, might be found unto praise and honor and glory at the appearing of Jesus Christ:" I Peter 1:7

1. How has your prayer life changed after reading this book?

2. What will you do differently when you pray for yourself or for others?

3. How will you share what you have learned?

Chapter 17

BNW — Weapons of Mass Destruction

ARE YOU AWARE you have three weapons of mass destruction to destroy the enemy? Do you know how to use them?

The Word clearly defines these weapons and our authority to apply them. Every believer has the same weapons for any area of our lives.

The first weapon is the blood — the precious blood of Jesus. The blood of Jesus is the covering that gives us the authority to use the other two weapons — the Name and the Word.

These three weapons work together. Each one is powerful in itself, but we must first understand our authority and use the weapons of mass destruction God has provided for us.

Christ shed His blood not just for our protection against sin when we received him into our hearts, but also for our healing.

We can pray, "I am protected because of the blood that Jesus shed, and when You took those stripes on your body for every major disease, 39 stripes, 39 major diseases it was for my healing, and not just my salvation."

The blood covers our salvation, our healing, and our deliverance. We can walk free because of that precious blood of Jesus.

Second Weapon – Name of Jesus

Our second weapon of mass destruction is the Name of Jesus. But, as with any weapon, there must be an authority behind it. When we understand our authority in Christ and the power of attorney He has given us to use His Name, we will approach prayer from a new position.

Sometimes people will just 'throw' in the Name of Jesus as a formula for answered prayer. But we must comprehend when Christ died on the cross He said, "It is finished."

He had completed what God had promised. It is now up to us, as believers, to grasp that truth and pray thankfully that Jesus paid the price for us.

Whatever we are praying for we have the right to use those scriptures which are God's will because God's will is His Word.

Take that Word, express it with your mouth, get it deep into your heart, and pray "Father, your Word says, I have the right to expect this because of what Jesus did for me. I have the right to use the name of Jesus in this situation and to come against anything the enemy would try to put on me."

We have that right. The Name of Jesus is above every other name. His Name is above fear, it is above sickness, and it is above disease. It is above strife and it is above anxiety.

It is above everything negative we could think of that we may come against in our life.

We have the right to use the name of Jesus against those things that would try to destroy us and speak to it with God-given authority.

Fear, you have no right here. "God has not given me the spirit of fear but of power and love and soundness of mind" 2 Timothy 1:7.

Find the scripture that addresses your need, pray the scripture, and get it into your heart. Then it becomes life in us; it is quickened in us and becomes the Rhema Word, which is the Word of God spoken directly from His mouth to our spirit.

We know that God is true to His Word. And He has given us the right to use his Name.

Jesus was born of God and was God. He exercised His authority by birthright. We are created by God and granted the authority that Jesus had, not by birthright but by proxy, when we ask in Jesus' name. Jesus said to ask in His name, and He will do it. He was giving His power of attorney.

"Whatever you ask in My name, that I will do, that the Father may be glorified in the Son. If you ask anything in My name, I will do it" John 14:14.

As Jesus spoke to Phillip in John 14:10 "Do you not believe that I am in the Father and the Father in Me? The words that I speak to you I do not speak on my own authority, but the Father who dwells in Me does the works."

Our relationship with Jesus is our legal basis for our authority but only to the extent that it expresses God's will — which is His Word.

And when we grasp that authority that is God-given, we can stand against any adversity and use the Name of Jesus to destroy the enemy.

Realize deeply that we have the Word of God in us, in our spirit. We can know beyond any doubt or any fear that tries to ensnare us that we are victorious because of that precious Name.

So when we use that Name, when we understand the authority behind that Name, we know by faith that we can do what we need to do to destroy the works of the enemy in any situation.

We have that document, we have that power of attorney, we have that authority, and we have God-given anointing in us to overtake, overrun, and overrule anything the enemy would try to put on us.

Authority to Be In Command

The name of Jesus is a weapon of mass destruction when we understand what is behind that Name and the authority we are given to use it.

Philippians 2:9 assures us that EVERYTHING is subject to the name of Jesus.

- Sickness is subject to the Name

- Terror and Fear are subject to the Name

- Pain is subject to the Name

The Name of Jesus is above all names and gives us the AUTHORITY TO BE IN COMMAND. The anointing is the empowerment of authority.

Third Weapon of Mass Destruction — Word of God

The third weapon of mass destruction we have is the Word of God. His Word, on our lips, controls the enemy.

The Word is our authority. It will destroy the works of the enemy. The Word on our lips makes the enemy the victim-- not us. The Word is what Jesus used against the enemy. When he was tempted, He didn't bargain with him, He used the Word.

Did you grasp the power of that statement? The Word of God, on our lips, controls the enemy. Stop speaking defeat to yourself by recognizing the negatives in your life and giving Satan credit for it.

Yes, you heard me correctly. When we confess with our mouths that the enemy has been working against us or when we define the battle we are having because of what he has thrown in our path, we are giving Satan the recognition he desperately wants. He regards it as praise, and he is thankful you see what he is doing in our lives.

But when the Word of God is on our lips and we are praising God that we are victors because of what Christ did on the cross, the enemy flees. He cannot stand to be in the presence of praise to our Heavenly Father.

What happened when Jesus was tempted by Satan? Did He argue with him? Did he try to reason with him? Did he cast him out? Jesus used one weapon. And that was the Word.

But don't kid yourself, the enemy probably knows the Word better than most of us. And he uses the Word to try to twist it. But Jesus knew the Word better. And He stuck with what the Word said. He didn't twist it. He didn't change it. He confirmed it. When we realize the power Jesus gave us to use the Word of God against any situation that we may be in, we will be victors, instead of victims.

What Happens When You Pray the Word

I have heard many people say, "Well, I prayed the Word, I believed the Word, but nothing happened."

My question to them is, "So why did you stop?"

If you truly believe that God has given you His Word and all the authority behind it, then you will understand that the timing is in God's hands – not yours.

"Blessed is she who believed, for there will be a fulfillment of those things which were told her from the Lord" Luke 1:45.

God gave me His promise from Luke 1:45 for my healing from uterine cancer. I refused to allow doubt, fear, circumstances, or a timeline to interfere with that promise. I saw the fulfillment of that promise fourteen years later when I gave birth to our daughter. I continue to thank God for His promise.

I thanked Him that His timing was perfect.

Many years later, I am continuing to see how God's timing was flawless. Yes, it was difficult to wait for years but I kept my focus on the promise instead of the problem. My focus never changed, and I saw the fulfillment of that promise. And I understand it more all the time.

We must grasp that Word, that promise, in our spirit. Head knowledge of the scriptures (the Logos or written Word) is not the Rhema Word. The Rhema Word is spoken to our hearts from the mouth of God. There is a quickening in our spirit when we hear that Word from God. The scripture comes alive. We know that we know that we know that God has spoken His Word to our hearts, and we can bank on it.

The Rhema Word comes alive in us. It removes all doubt. It excites us. We can almost taste it — it is so tangible.

When we are begging God and hoping, wishing, and wondering, that is not standing on the living, spoken Word of God to our hearts. And doubt and fear can rob us of that promise.

But Jesus understood the authority behind the spoken Word of God. He spoke it out with confidence knowing in His Spirit that God would fulfill what He promised.

When that scripture is in our spirit and we stand firm on it with all the authority of God behind it, we will realize that we are in the arena of faith. We will see Satan as the defeated victim.

It is also important to remember that if we consistently recognize and give credit to the enemy and what he is trying to do — we are, in essence, praising him. He loves to be recognized and takes pride in it.

But when we learn to recognize God in every situation instead, we can approach any situation from a positive position, rather than from a place of defeat.

When we complain about the things that are going wrong, the attacks we feel we are facing, and the fear in a situation, we are providing fertile territory for the devil to play games with our state of mind. Remember that the anointing in you from God is far greater than anything the devil throws at you. That authority has been given to you along with your right to use the name of Jesus to destroy the works of the enemy.

The anointing is ours. The anointing is upon us when Jesus came in via His Holy Spirit and is dwelling in our spirit. The empowerment of that anointing gives us the authority to take a stand against the things that would try to destroy us.

Take a moment to thank God for the anointing on your life that reigns in you because of Jesus. Start by turning your prayers of petition into prayers of praise. Thank God that the name of Jesus is ABOVE every other name — the name of sickness, disease, fear, or loss is subject to the name of Jesus.

We have the right to pray with authority and anointing – we don't have to beg God but rather thank Him for what He has provided.

We thank You, Lord, that You have given us that authority with the anointing of your Spirit Who dwells within our spirit. We can stand on the Word which is yes and amen. And we can say, "Sickness be gone, disease be gone, pain be gone in the name of Jesus." Choose to believe the Word of God. And watch what happens.

B — Blood of Jesus
N — Name of Jesus
W — Word of God

1. **Are you ready to make a change in your prayer life by using BNW?**

2. **Will you commit to taking time to study each weapon and realize it is not a formula.....but a way of life?**

Author's Bio

Carol Graham is an award-winning author, keynote speaker, prayer coach, teacher, podcaster, YouTuber, and dog rescuer. She is a master charismatic storyteller whose message is passionate and uplifting. With riveting true stories, Carol conveys how to overcome doubt, fear, trauma, and everything in between. She is an expert in surviving against all odds.

Carol Graham received the **Woman of Impact Award** and **Author of the Year** for her memoir, *Battered Hope*, and the global award for **One Woman — Fearless** which is given to women who have faced their fears and made the world a better place.

Your questions and comments are important to me.
I would love to connect with you.
Please contact me at:

Email: carolg4589@gmail.com
Website: prayingmiracles.com
YouTube: PrayingForMiraclesWithCarol